Verse of Life

Verse of Life

Joel David Kilgore

Joel David Kilgore
2023

First Printing: 2023

ISBN 978-1-961629-03-5

Joel David Kilgore
P.O. Box 1271
Manassas, VA 20108

Dedication

The contents of this book are dedicated to:

Every reciepitant of the gift itself. God granted this gift of poetry for his purpose. Mine is just to write unconditionally and not impede the spirit.

To God for trusting me with gift of poetry that calls unto his spirit and binds itself into the lives of the readers.

Contents

Acknowledgements

God has bestowed a gift of poetry upon me. This is certainly not a brag, it is not a burden, it is a passion. I am passionate about the gift. The gift, however, is not for me. It is literally for everyone else.

About the Author

Joel David Kilgore has been writing poetry for over four decades. What started as a prayer of faith blossomed to a spiritual burden to carry out and complete. However, writing poetry of this kind is never complete because in his understanding, derives from God's spirit which is never-ending. Many of the poems in the book were personally handed to recipients through greeting cards, in a signed book, or in an email as a word of encouragement.

At the early age of 16 years old Joel prayed for the gift of poetry. At the same age Joel was called to the front of a church service he was attending under H Richard Hall and ordained as a Pentecostal Holiness minister. The ordination spurred a spiritual fire within Joel that fed a flame within him to minister. However, Joel took a different course in life and served in the US Air Force as a Telecommunications Technician for 22 years. The desire to minister never diminished, but instead, re-emerged within the gift of poetry. Within these texts, the passion for ministry combined with the spiritual gift of poetry, springs life within the verses that praises, encourages, inspires, and transcends God's essence to the reader. Although Joel feels he cannot take any credit for the poetry due to it being a gift from God, he acknowledges being obedient to the gift.

Joel has often said that it is difficult, at times, to write if he isn't around people. This claim, in his understanding, is that God's spirit within people dictate the poem. If there is no one in spiritual need, then he does often feel a burden to write poetry. And yet he feels every soul is burdened to a point of seeking delivery, even his own. In The Holy Bible, Romans 3:23 "For all have sinned, and come short of the glory of God;" In Joel's view, no one except Jesus Christ can ever be perfect. All else are imperfect in their own way. To this end, all imperfections are made perfect through God's spirit. The poetry he writes, if deemed perfect by any reader, is only perfect through the spirit of God. If there is one impression that he can leave by publishing poetry, it is for the reader to pick up their bible, read, and pray.

Preface

At an early age of 16 years old I prayed in faith to Christ for the ability to write poetry. Not just any poetry, but a gift that would bind hearts back to God and explain God's mysteries. I never wanted to receive credit for any of the writings, but rather wanted to acknowledge that the gift was from God, and he only should receive any recognition for any poem received. God answered the prayer, and I began to write. When writing begins I feel an inward draw to document the poem. It is as if the poem is being born and is alive, but also has always existed. The draw, or rather God's spirit's call "pulls" at my spirit, and I generally hear only the first few words as I begin to write. What follows is the rest of the poem, word-by-word, and line-by-line. I cannot change the writings nor forcibly try to write. With that reasoning, I do not feel that I am the true author for any of the poems within this book. God is the true author, and I am merely the vessel of delivery for these texts.

I thank God for his spirit, I thank God for his presence, and I thank God for his gifts.

Introduction

This is the second compilation of poetry in association with "The Spirit's Call." Although most poems are written in a first-person singular fashion, they were in fact written for specific individuals in what I can only label as their spirit's voice. If the poem indicates the writer to be a specific gender, keep in mind that the poem was written as I heard God's spirit speak.

If any of the readers of this small book can find a word of encouragement, then it is very worth all the effort in compiling and publishing. The gifts from God are not driven or owned by the recipients, but rather a charge to acknowledge and let them manifest and minister in the spirit of the gift. God allowed me a gift of poetry, and I pray to always keep in mind and heart that the gift is not for my benefit, but for and to those of whom the spirit of God touches.

This book is a compilation of the poems written to or for individuals, in prayer or praise to God, or just in general. The poems in this book were written for various occasions and a variety of subjects. All poems are listed by title, in alphabetical order.

There are a few poems that spell out the title or a message by reading the first letter or word of every line. God has allowed some creativity, but not so much as to detract from the poem's message. If these poems are not obvious in that they have a hidden text, turn to the last section titled "Hidden Texts" for a guide to their locations.

Joel David Kilgore

Verse of Life

The Absolute

Life is full of wishes
Life is full of woes,
Life is full of maybes
Life will come and go,

Life is full of hard times
Life is full of sad,
Life is full of happy
Life is full of glad,

Life can have some misery
Life can have some fun,
Life has a beginning
And also, its end run,

Life is full of questions
Some of never asked,
Life is full of burdens
Life is full of tasks,

If there is tomorrow
As much as is today,
Life will be repeating
In all of its known ways,

Life is of abundance
When with God we choose,
Life is then fulfilling
Of which we cannot lose,

Life is full of answers
To questions never asked,
If we ask God to guide us
And do his bidding task,

Life is then rewarding
In all we choose to do,
When we acknowledge God's life
Life is absolute.

A Friend

A friend of mine I know his name
He knows of me and would be fame,

His heart of gold I do surmise
As world is seen through his eyes,

I put to task a little thing
And to the world some prose to bring,

And yet I lacked upon the thought
To let all, see what Spirit caught,

Then my friend held me to task
To give to all of what I asked,

For what I asked was not for me
But for all to read and see,

Now the task is just ere done
And can be seen by everyone!

A Higher Cause

It seems men seek to destroy souls
Make haste to war to win their goals,

We praise ourselves for being best
We seek a challenge, need a test,

We choose to live a life of strife
With foes, with friends, and with our wives,

Such a time as we now live in
As hearts do seek unwilling sin,

 To each his own, to each his will
We say with tongue proclaim with quill,

"It is my rite; I am I am"
As Spirit bids this thought "I am,"

"We are right and else is wrong"
It is seen high, it's sung in song,

"Follow us as we will win"
But what of strife and what of sin?

Nations rise to reach their cause
Make their boundaries with their cause,

Poets write in blinding haste
What time is this? - Is life a waste?

It's time to look, to turn, to see
A higher cause of you and me,

If man would be a godly form
Destruction to us all,

Since God has taken manly form
May grace upon us fall.

A Little Dove

A symbol of God's spirit
A snow-white turtle dove,
We loftily see it flying
In the skies above,

In whiteness it is holy
In oils it is quite blessed,
In flight it is of spirit
It symbolizes rest,

For God and all his labors
Chose this little dove,
To end the plight of Noah
And use this sign for love,

Such a little token
To teach us all so well,
That God can use a small thing
To of his story tell,

The Holy Ghost in spirit
Is symbolled like a dove,
And God with all his blessings
Will use this dove as love,

Of all the other creatures
There's none so pure we find,
That tells us of the master
Who made all living kind.

A Mother's Wish

It started many months ago
That I began this child,
I feel it grow inside of me
So tender and so mild,

I think often that it's there
And what shall I become?
A mother with one innocent
And how to raise this one?

I feel my youth has slipped away
And I've become a child,
Not knowing from each day to day
Of how to raise one mild,

What kind of mother will I be?
Will I come to tears?
What of this child am I to see?
Will I endure all fears?

As a mother soon to be
I do have my doubts,
I doubt my wisdom caries through
In all the ins and outs,

Perhaps it's wisdom that I seek
Of that I should pray,
To teach this child of life itself
And how to meet each day,

I pray to God he hears my prayer
And answers it each day,
So, I may show my child great love
And unto God to pray.

A Prayer of Faith

With each word I hear and say
I find a meaning in,
To make a point of meaningness
To cry aloud and win,

If I choose to say a word
Or if I choose to smile,
My word of truth comes from within
My smile comes of my style,

In this life we seldom hear
Our spirits inner cry,
The words of which, speak to God
They never form a lie,

If we choose to follow God
Then always we're in prayer,
We feel his smile and soft rebuke
We always know he's there,

So, when you pray think this wise
God will always hear,
He knows the thoughts of hearts and minds
And He is always near,

If you pray, please pray in faith
For he will know your heart,
And always know that he prayed first
From God we'll never part.

A Thoughtful Word

The hours that we're given
In any given day,
Are hours of our living
Of all we do, we say,

Will we speak of wisdom
Of faith, or truest love?
Will we speak religion
Or speak to God above?

Will our hearts be loyal
To what we feel is close?
Will we hold our heart true
To what we love the most?

The answers to these questions
Are never hard to find,
It's what we choose to utter
From our hearts and minds.

A Wish for Mom

Every time I go away
I wish that I had stayed,
A little longer by your side
Often, I had prayed,

It seems that I should know you more
I hold your heart so dear,
Every day I see you mom
These thoughts are e'er more clear,

I thank God for your thoughtfulness
I thank him for your love,
For your caring heart's caress
And your faith to God above,

Today I pass to you one wish
From my heart's truest form,
I pray you have the sweetest day
Since time when you were born.

All Saints Holy

All saints serve the savior
They give their heart to God,
They relish prayerful moments
They feel God's spirit nod,

They listen for his heartbeat
Within his holy word,
They pray he will their souls keep
Through words of faith they heard,

They fast and are not weary
They work and will not faint,
They give their lives to all men
They live the life of saint,

These saints, they are the Christians
Who in their hearts believe,
The words of our Lord Jesus
And of him they receive,

In spirit, they're in sainthood
In life, they're in our lives,
In history, they're in writings
They're always in God's eyes,

If you ever meet one
You will know it's true,
They are of All Saints Holy
Because that's what they do.

All Things Living

Every breath ever taken
From creatures under sun,
Are not gone and not forsaken
In essence they are one,

God has formed all living creatures
To be a help to man,
He made their lives and all their features
With the voice of his command,

Ever small or ever heavy
These creatures are to be,
Is what God sought to levy
These creatures that we see,

Every moment of our living
On this Earth we stand,
We must know of God's own giving
To us - - in every land,

God has formed all creatures for us
At first, in jubilee,
By Adam's fall in Eden's chorus
These creatures from us flee,

Now we use them for to nourish
Our living essence be,
Instead of letting them all flourish
We eat them hum-b-ly,

Heaven's creatures won't be eaten
Not by any man,
But there in morning and the evening
The Lion lays with Lamb.

Always

Pamela, today is very special
Have fun and laughter too,
A time for you to relax
Wonderful moments meant for you,

Birthday wishes all around
Season greetings of the occasion,
And just in case no one else said
"Enjoy every sensation,"

Every day I think of you
Minute, after minute,
I'm preparing a small gift for you
Sending this card as well within it,

This may seem but trivial
. . . message in a card,
With every line in which you read
More is seen if you read hard,

Love is more than I can say
Than what I always feel,
I simply cannot e'er express
Can you tell these words are real?

Express is but a minor task
In what I know to do,
Written in God's holy book
Or by his spirit true,

Spoken words are not enough
Words, I feel that I must say,
Love is bursting in my heart
You probably know that today,

Always,
David

Amantes Graviditate

I feel you there inside me
As you gently move around,
With silent times behind me
A joy in earth I've found,

I know when you're awakened
And just can't fall asleep,
Your restlessness reminds me
Of cautions I should keep,

This feeling is quite daunting
Of what you are to be,
You see my little darling
You are a part of me,

Your presence has assured me
That God does hold all plans,
I feel the love of loving
Why God created man,

The moments that astound me
Are when I feel you there,
It gives me peace assurance
Of you - - I'm taking care,

Your presence there has changed me
To see this world anew,
I cannot wait to see you
And see the thing you do,

My sights have changed profoundly
Of what I see in man,
And all that is around me
Of what I know I am,

I wait for you my darling
To hold you in my care,
And keep you safely always
You have my love to share,

So, when you're finally here child
I'll be what I should be,
A kind and loving mother
To this child that I shall see.

Amina Rose Fisher

Always in my heart
My little baby girl,
I learn from her each day
Now time will pass and whirl,

All she says and does
Reminds me much of me,
Of things that I would do
Such things in her I see,

Every day I know
From watching what she sees,
I'm in this little girl
She is a part of me,

Her life has saved my own
Each day I know that true,
Really, I must say
My daughter - - I love you.

The Angel in My Arms

She sleeps, she cries, she murs, she coos
Her infant feet can't yet wear shoes,
Her eyes behold me as I look
She cuddles fast when reading books,

She takes my heart to worlds away
I hear her cries and make them fade,
My heart beats twice when her I see
This angel sweet as she can be,

Her every whence, my every breath
Her every move puts me to test,
I see the world now fresh and new
To us, newborns, of this will do,

All I thought of what I knew
Changed when bonds of child came through,
Now that world has washed away
This angel brings a whole new day.

Anticipations

For all anticipations
There is a civil rest,
When all our reservations
Are at our conscious best,

When we all know the reasons
All our sins and strife,
Yield unto the season
That gives to us all life,

When e'er were at this juncture
We know who holds all love,
It's held by Christ our savior
Who watches from above.

Appreciation

All the reasons I find in life
To live from day to day,
I find great joy in things I love
And they are here to stay,

The love of family kin and friends
It soars mu soul to heights,
To know the kinships will not end
It keeps my soul from freights,

I love my country grand and strong
I'm proud to be within it,
To make it safe for all within
I'll serve with pride and own it,

The things that God has treasured most
Is all of his creation,
Nature's cast is handed down
And is in every nation,

All that God has given us
We are here to tend,
And keep all safe within this life
Until all time will end.

Ara Aloise Nash Friedberg

Ara my little angel
Rest for now and sleep,

All the time I waited
All the time to keep,

Looking at you softly
On the little bed,

I know that all my waiting
Sure leaves something said,

Every moment pondered
Nearly took my breath,

As your near appearing
Stayed upon my chest,

How you take my heartbeat
From when I saw your face,

Really makes me happy
I feel my pulses race,

Every day I carried
Does not e'er compare,

Because you are my baby
Each moment we will share,

Rest for now my angel...
...going fast asleep.

The Ardent Wake

Decades come and swiftly pass
As life goes on and lost loves last,
Spirits near and spirits far
Call our hearts to who we are,

Silently as souls run deep
Our love will grow as others sleep,
Seep they will from out our midst
No more to tempt us, we resist,

Our hearts merry in our dreams
Within our lives in our schemes,
We give notion to ourselves
Of others, have our spirits shelved,

Unto God, we have one plea
Keep us safe in harmony,
Let not one of other tempt
Let our love shine as we are kept,

Let our marriage be of cheer
Holding each closely dear,
Knowing that there is no other
That we would have as each our lover.

The Art of Holy Living

The art of holy living
Not looking at the past,
But reaches for tomorrow
And all that ever lasts,

To live and love in lifetime
To hold all loved ones dear,
To grasp the ever after
To love without life's fear,

To know that God's tomorrow
Holds promise of today,
To give unto us wisdom
As we traverse our way,

And grants His Holy Spirit
To reach into our lives,
To lift us yet much higher
To His clearest skies,

The art of holy living
Is in a single prayer,
To ask and then be faithful
That God will meet you there.

Astronaverse

Twinkle goes the little star
Its height is beyond man,
Yet try man does to reach its height
And tries like no one can,

A light year is a life away
Of which no man can reach,
With travels that we have today
We can only teach,

We teach of things that rise at night
Of which we barely see,
Of stars that twinkle, oh so bright
We wonder what they be,

We look with scopes to find a way
If we could only touch,
The surface of the things we see
We would learn so much,

Quasars, stars, the galaxies
The hosted, celestial choir,
The rings and moons of planets vast
We look and we admire,

If we could only once to go
To a planet far,
We'd find new hope in doing so
To touch the stellar star,

Perhaps in time we shall see
A planet much like ours,
And treat it with respect of life
Instead of what devours.

The Attendant

Cars do come and cars do go
On any given day,
Of every make and model
Seem to come my way,

The reasons for the visit
May not be so clear,
But true I always see them
Throughout entire year,

Some for business, some for fun
Some for just an hour,
Some will take up residence
Some of esteemed power,

If you come to visit
This parking space I have,
You're sure to see things near it
And of them speak and gab,

All who come to see me
With cars of great and small,
I'll extend a welcome
And take care of you all,

To some of great importance
To some that time's forgot,
But all are surely welcome
That park within my lot.

Aunt Tenice – The Traveler

Decades came and went away
As May lived her life,
She has a loving sister
A mother, sorts, a wife,

She lived a life of fullness
She loved a daily brew,
She loved all pets she could find
Yet she owned so few,

A mother sorts she came to be
Yet bore none her own,
But cared for them as they were hers
She took them to her home,

She celebrated life so dear
Of all the freedoms given,
A celebration once a year
Of that our Nation's living,

She loved to visit other lands
She travelled to them far,
To see how others lived their lives
She went by plane and car,

She lived this life of fullness
Fore ore a century grand,
Seeing distant countries
And living in this land,

She opened mediation
To those who could not see,
That life was full of virtue
Of things to do and see,

We'll miss her mediations
The way she lived her life,
This special sorts of mother
This loving sister, wife,

Somewhere in the distant
On some celestial shore,
May is still receiving
And travelling once more.

*In Memory of
Mary Veronica Dean
May 10, 1915 – March 27, 2019*

Bang!

A shot rang out, a mother cried
On local news her child had died,
A man and gun played out death's toll
So many died both young and old,

This story goes, repeats again
It claims the lives of family, friends,
We want to blame both man and gun
But rarely blame where all begun,

We watch our shows, we see the man
Makes body counts with gun in hand,
We make them heroes on silver screen
While killing men, of story, mean,

Our children sit and play the game
Of killing sport, of more the same,
We find the toys upon store shelves
That teaches child of guns themselves,

For every person there is a start
That introduced to each their part,
If I recall, to me first rang
As little child, I said: "bang-bang,

Bang, bang-bang-bang, bang!"

Better Days

On better days and at my worst
I did not lie in bed,
Recovering from doctors cut
I had my joys instead,

Here I lie with stitch up wound
I had to take the knife,
To take the pain away from me
And give me better life,

Now I find myself to say
I'd wish this on no one,
The pain and stitched recovery
Is not the least of fun,

If you take a sec or two
And ask what was the matter?
I'll look at you and tell you true
They took out my gall bladder.

Blessed

God has blessed me
Lovingly so,
Our praises to Him
Richly they flow,

I reach to please Him
As I seek to pray,
During this life
As I find my way,

Nothing can hinder
in this walk I seek,
Everything is for me
Love is to keep,

Look unto Him
Everywhere is He,
Keep your faith high
In your heart you'll see,

Laughter and joy
Goes hand in hand,
O'er all ages
Reserved for man,

Evermore praising
I give Him my all,
Love, joy, and laughter
You hear my heart's call.

Blessed is The Lord

Blessed is the Lord for he is holy
Blessed is the Lord for he is pure,
Blessed is the Lord for he is righteous
Blessed is the Lord for he is sure,

I feel his spirit near me
When I kneel down to pray,
I feel that he is watching
What e'er I do and say,

Blesses is the Lord for he is worthy
Blessed is the Lord for he is light,
Blessed is the Lord for he is mighty
Blessed is the Lord day and night,

I hear his spirit calling
"My child come unto me,"
I feel my spirit falling
To be as he would be,

Blessed is the Lord the Christ and Savior
Blessed is the Lord who saves us all,
Blessed is the Lord of all living
Blessed is the Lord on him I call,

I feel he is around me
All throughout the day,
His angels do surround me
And guide me on my way,

Blessed is the Lord my God almighty
Blesses is the Lord at heaven's stand,
Blessed is the Lord for he is watching
And rules the universe with his command,

I know that God is with us
And guides us on our way,
If we will but serve him
Yield to him and pray,

Blessed is the Lord the mighty master
Who rules the earth with love unfeigned divine,
Blessed is the lord for he is mighty
And shall be in all eternal time.

The Blossom

Summer, Spring, Winter, Fall
Four seasons and we know them all,
Summer's hot, Winter's cold
With Spring we're young, with Fall we're old,

Every Spring new life we see
We feel the warmth, we see new leaves,
We hear the birds; they chirp and fly
We see new life that fills the sky,

We see the seeds from Autumn's plant
Spring to life with Spring's new chant,
We see the flowers of the trees
Their pollen sought of honeybees,

With each new life that we see grow
In it is God, we see Him sow,
The earth lives new as spring comes on
We love this time, of it we're fond,

With every Summer, Winter Spring
We see life in different things,
When fall arrives we see things die
We wish for spring and cheery skies,

Of all the things that God has done
We wish for spring to be the one,
Of what we see and what we feel
We know this time of life is real,

The blossoming of this season
Leads us to joy and newer reason,
The joy of Spring within our land
Makes us sure, we're in God's hand.

The Bonding

When I first beheld your eyes
And looked into your face,
I felt my heart tremble so
I knew I'd seen God's grace,

He blessed me with your lovely life
A gift from heaven high,
I praised him from that moment on
And felt his spirit sigh,

The beauty of this little girl
I held within my arms,
Throughout my life to keep you safe
And free from all life's harms,

The world about me changed that day
No longer was I me,
But part of me was in my arms
In this little face I see,

I opened up my heart that day
To keep you there within,
So. my daughter as you know
I am your father - - but always your friend.

The Business

People come and go
They visit every day,
They purchase what they want
Of what they wish to pay,

Open to their needs
Of what we have on hand,
We make them meals of great
From a foreign land,

We use our expertise
To prepare every day,
To make the tasty bites
As we will do our way,

So, if you happen by
And choose a tasty meal,
Know it's from our heart
That's why the tastes are real.

Called Home

When shadows fall around us
And the sunlight fades away,
The dark clouds come and gather
As the darkness breaks the day,

And the view of our surroundings
Seem to gently slip away,
As our faith it seems to flounder
When our eyesight is dismayed,

When e'er I came to see you
And I thought you would be there,
My soul found something missing
It was much for me to bear,

Yet the silence of surroundings
Of the words I could not hear,
Was you're voice so softly sounding
Of why you were not there,

The calling from the master
Of every living thing,
Had called you home forever
To the heavens as they ring.

In Memory of
William O. Newman
October 19, 1937 - February 5, 2017

The Chairs

Today we sit and see ourselves
Next to our warming hearth,
We've lived a life of fullness
Till now back to our birth,

We count these days as blessings
God gave to us to live,
In giving, I find we give back
A testament to live,

Our hours are filled with passing
From time to given time,
To make each day e'er lasting
With rhythm and its rhyme,

The things we do in life we share
This is our time to keep,
To hold each other ever close
Awake or when we sleep,

As age creeps near upon us
We sit in humble chairs,
We watch our glowing hearth of warmth
And think about life's cares,

The beauty of our moments
Is not just what you see,
But knowing that God framed our lives
To what we now can be.

Chapter Two

My life is full of wishes
Of things that I would do,
Many of which I've done
I've seen both old and new,

Me and just my Mrs.'s
Will take a holiday,
Both long and extensive
We will move away,

Away from all the hustle
The politics, the crime,
Away from heavy traffic
To another place we'll find,

To our imaginations
We will seek new life,
Where solitude will find us
Just me and lovely wife,

Of golden years folks wait for
We'll start ours early on,
And wake with each new day for
The things that we are fond,

We'll take our living treasures
And move them down the road,
And really live each day for
The things in heart we hold,

In life, we all live chapters
The first of working man,
With sweat of tears and eyebrow
He does his work's command,

This will be our chapter
To make our life anew,
"What chapter?" you'll be asking
We're living Chapter Two.

Cherish

I listened to the news today
A different frame of mind,
I heard of women suffrage
Of what is so unkind,

The thing I cannot fathom
Is how this came to be?
To treat another human
So un-respectingly,

Why do men treat women
As victims of desire?
Why do they disgrace them
And set both souls on fire?

One to be the victim
Of what is never love,
The other held in judgement
Of God, who sees above,

How is it that this daunting
That pains our world today,
Still exists among us?
And will not go away?

Can it be that somehow
We will see the way?
To cherish souls more closely
With what we do and say?

Perhaps we'll find the answer
If we seek God above,
And understand the meaning
Of how that God - - is love.

The Child

In early hours of morning
I wake to days of mild,
To some days ever stressing
To thoughts of newborn child,

Yet in my meditations
Of which I tame my thoughts,
I thank God for his blessings
Of what this Child has brought,

It brings me joy in knowing
That it is part of me,
And part is of the father
Of what this child will be,

And as the day approaches
That this child is in my arms,
Where I will safely keep it
From all ill will and harms,

So, knowing I'm the mother
Of what this child will be,
I'll keep it in my heart of love
Throughout eternity.

Children of Time

Once a time – a gathering
Of spirits, souls and minds,
Memories of happiness
Of poems, loves, and rhymes,

We were young and we were bold
To make our lives anew,
A jest, a jab, a word in time
We loved all that we'd do,

Moments passed and seasons changed
Our ways, they found new paths,
We found ourselves yet questioning
Things we had failed to ask,

Within our lives came misery
With happiness and woes,
Still, we held to memories
As each our story goes,

Moments more had slipped away
We found ourselves again,
Relations new, relations old
Yet still, we were good friends,

As the days had lingered on
Moments turned to years,
We laughed and cried with bitterness
With happy thoughts and tears,

In life's journey all is naught
Except for loves and loss,
We make our path with surety
And often pay the cost,

We plan our days with simpleness
We take our nights with care,
We hold to each with lovingness
In hopes we're always there,

This story is for all of us
So please keep this in mind,
You're in this story that I tell
Of Earth's -- Children of Time.

The Christ

In a manger He laid
As wise men looked on,
To honor this babe
Of whom they were fond,

He grew to age twelve
And taught to the scribes,
The just ways of God
And where God abides,

Then came He a man
He called to His own,
To seek and to save
He came from God's throne,

He fed them with fish
He fed them with loaves,
He fed of His word
He fed them in droves,

He gave them the light
The light of all men,
The light of God's might
Which freed them from sin,

He walked for three years
To carry His word,
And many it freed
All that had heard,

He gave them a life
Which would not die,
Or ever would pass
As end proaches nigh,

He lifted his life
To free every soul,
To heal them of ill
And cleanse them all whole,

In all that we do
And all that we see,
If we see this Christ
He'll set us to, free,

There's nothing to lose
But all life to gain,
By serving Him true
And knowing His pain,

If e'er we decide
To turn and to see,
He'll give us His life
And set our souls free,

It just takes one prayer
To know Him e'er true,
And change all our life
To what he would do,

So, Christ in our heart
His words in our head,
His comfort and guidance
We'll never be dead,

But into His kingdom
We'll find our souls free,
From all this life's trials
We'll serve Him with glee,

So, in this lost world
Of poetry prose,
Just reach unto God
For your heart - - He knows.

The Colors of Life

In moments so brief
In darkness of night,
In sunshine filled days
In seconds of fright,

In words that we think
In things that we say,
In books that we read
In theatrical plays,

In songs that are played
In poetic prose,
In splendor of heavens
In petals of rose,

In hues that we see
In feelings of love,
In disdain and hate
In heaven above,

The time of our living
In love, wrath, or strife,
All bring unto us
The colors of life.

Claim the Day

I'd like to think the job I do
Is from my heart within,
Cause with a flare I do it well
Be it good or sin,

I skate my way throughout my day,
Working as I must,
I do not play in this stay
You can surely trust,

In play I'd be some miles from here
Down in Dominican way,
And there enjoy the beach and sun
It's so fun I must say,

But still, I am a patriot
Of this country fine,
Born on Independence Day you see
I enjoy freedoms time,

If you see me having fun
And like the shoes I wear,
There's more at home where they came from
I have plenty there,

Whether playing, working hard
Or laying on the beach,
I'll be good at what I do
Perfection I will reach,

So, if you happen by one day
And see me at my best,
Know for sure that all or none
Each day is like the rest,

Each day of life is precious
Each hour I find the time,
To enjoy every moment
And make the day be mine.

The Compass

Every man has sorrow
And every soul has glee,
We all look to tomorrow
We all look to be free,

Every day's a journey
Every chore's a care,
Every breath is gifted
We live because we dare,

Every night's a mission
To make it to the morn,
Every dream's a lesson
As through our life it's worn,

Every person speaking
Will speak a word of care,
Every person working
Has something there to share,

Every moment passing
Will lead into the next,
Of futures, present and history past
And be in recorded texts,

Life's a spinning cycle
Which has no start nor end,
As we travel through it
We meet family, foe, and friend,

If all our lives meaning
Could be summed upon a page,
The page would reach unto the stars
And change with age to age,

The truth of our existence
Is from the Lord on high,
With Him we'll find its meaning
If we'll but only try,

So, reach into tomorrow
To find it is today,
And know that all life's sorrows
With God, will have no stay,

In this little message
With simple rhyme and verse,
Has arrows pointing up to God
Who reached down to us first.

Conceptual Time

Time is ever passing
As years will slip away,
Our thoughts are e'er surpassing
Of what time has to say,

All of life around us
Breathes of the same air,
All the folks about us
Have often same of cares,

In moments of time passing
We find we need more time,
To make the day more lasting
To do the things we find,

A moment never lingers
As all time slips away,
We often find our future
Is same as time today,

Perhaps if we once ponder
That time is of our choice,
Of what we choose to say and hear
And what we choose to voice,

Then time becomes no longer
Of what will slip away,
Instead. it makes us stronger
To meet each brand-new day.

Congressional Seat

A word to many congress folk
To us you have all Lied!
Dishonesty is your platform
And by God, you are despised!

You care not for the people
That placed you in that chair,
Instead, you stick to politics
And of your heart, don't care,

You run on lies in promise
To assist fellow man,
But once you've gained the office
You're anything but, "I Can,"

While we of woes and sorrows
You take away our lives,
You vote without a conscious
For laws that cause us strife,

You turn your eyes from reason
That helps your people true,
Then hide behind your party
In all the wrong you do,

It's past time for a cleaning
Of every membered seat,
From those that have no values
To those who will not cheat!

Conscious of Truth

I sat inside a court today
And listened to the truth,
In the case were witnesses
In this case was proof,

The case contained some characters
Of which would testify,
They uttered in great sentences
And would not tell a lie,

Their words were not for worldly gain
Nor for prosperity,
But rather not to tell a lie
Nor to e'er to deceive me,

Their conscious kept them free and clear
Of impropriety,
And made their case fair and strong
Just like a case should be.

The Cure

In faint my heart had wavered
I felt the sway within,
A weakness hit my body
I felt that I had sinned,

A momentary relapse
Of days that had gone by,
I thought that if just perhaps
That God would hear my cry,

I cried to God in anguish
To feel His calm resolve,
For all is made quite perfect
If God is thus involved,

I cried to Him for healing
That I should see less pain,
I asked He'd be revealing
Of who He is again,

I felt I knew the answer
As I knelt down to pray,
That God would heal thereafter
As my pain would be stayed,

That's when I heard the master
Of all life known to man,
He spoke of the hereafter
And all He would command,

To my err of knowledge
I thought my pain was mine,
But God told me He took it
By His son's cross divine,

Wounded for transgressions
Bruised for iniquities,
Our chastised peace upon Him
And by His stripes we're healed,

These words then found new meaning
God told this truth to me,
He asked that I believe Him
And of His will receive,

The faith of our forefathers
Was not just in the cross,
But in God's Holy Spirit
Which paid the curing cost.

The Dancer's Dance

In troubled nights of sorrow
In daytime's gleeful smile,
In yearning for tomorrow
I choose to dance a while,

In all of nature's meaning
In brightness of the day,
In celestials gleaming
Within the Milky Way,

A dance I see in daytime
With every blowing wind,
A dance I see at nighttime
In stars that never end,

I see myself e'er dancing
With all the breath I breathe,
In moments of romancing
And anguish to relieve,

In all life's truest meaning
I dance for love and friend,
I dance a dance of freedom
A dance that never ends,

If you see me dancing
You'll know my dancing way,
And yet I'm never chancing
To dance another day,

My dance is of my spirit
My moves are of my mind,
My song is simple vocal
I dance a dance that's mine,

I dance before tomorrow
I'll dance the night away,
I dance within my slumber
I dance when e'er I pray,

I dance the dancer's dancing
I dance the harmony,
I dance through trials and troubles
I dance a dance for me.

The Dawn of Days

In early man's beginnings
He met the Dawn of Days,
This Dawn created mankind
Set forth man in His ways,

He taught man of His wisdom
He kept man safe in care,
He let man know His virtue
He asked of man to share,

He let man know His glory
He taught man of His strength,
He told man of His presence
He holds all space immense,

He versed man of life's freedoms
Of sorrowed bitter woes,
Then asked man of Him to follow
Through all life's curves and throes,

To man He shared His spirit
To make a family high,
And keep man's heart so near it
Man joins Him if man dies,

This Dawn is Lord and savior
The blessed Son of God,
Who calls all souls unto Him
Where angels softly trod,

In life we know Christ's mercy
We pray to Him each day,
In death we know His spirit
Forsaking older ways,

When we pass this lifetime
How long or short the stay's,
We meet Christ in His glory
Therein the Dawn of Days.

In Memory of
Ignatius Armando Menezes
July 31, 1939 to May 2, 2018

The Day is Long

Early I rise to meet the day
With all my errand tasks,
Things to say, things to do
Things that may not last,

All my life has been the pace
From dawn to setting sun,
The things I find to do all day
Some daunting while some are fun,

There are moments that I find
Will pass so swiftly by,
Other moments seem as hours
Yet all moments with time flies,

You can ask me what I do
That takes up so much time,
But to tell you, I say true
I'd miss the tasks I find,

Just one day try to see
Follow as I go,
Then the meaning of these tasks
You will truly know,

It's not that I don't enjoy
Everything I do,
It's that I can't find the time
To see all tasks done thru.

Days Gone By

Today of days and years gone by
To this world you were born,
Unto a life full of dreams
Of which some have been torn,

But once we dream, we dream again
We bring our dreams to life,
By perseverance, sweat and prayers
Our dreams become our lives,

Our dream is broken, but not ourselves
Our dream is mere desire,
Our love for life is stronger than
The dream which won't transpire,

Years ago, a dream you dreamed
You know if it e'er was real,
But now today a life you live
That, in your heart you feel,

Today is the day you were born
Years and days gone by,
Thank God for all the days you've spent
And someday with him fly.

The Day's Values

Any measured living day
I find my soul at rest,
After work and family
Have put me to the test,

My family is the ultimate
They keep me fresh and new,
Work is what I have to do
I keep it in my view,

I'll relax when day is done
And all the tasks complete,
To tend to work, then family
I then can find relief.

Days of Summers Past

A gentle breeze on warm hot days
A whisper wind on mid-day haze,
A blowing leaf from trees aloft
A floaty cloud in skies so soft,

The days of summer years gone by
With views and storms from darkened skies,
The games we played out in the field
The times of life of which we'd yield,

The hours we spent awake at night
In summer's heat and heaven's light,
In heat of day and night's delight
Brought to us the summer's sight,

Years went by, we'd see the same
The heat, the night, the summer rain,
With each year we'd see this art
That God displayed, for our part,

Now today we've seen a turn
Of wind, of rain, of days that burn,
We yearn of days that time did cast
And wish for Days of Summers Past.

Dear Grandma, You Will Be Missed

In this life that is so short
I thank the Lord for being our escort,
These things I do believe in
Of love and joy between our God and men,
That on the day we may depart
And our loved one's brave heavy hearts,
That a multiple of warmth and peace awaits us,

The struggle and toil of living ends
And we journey on to rejoin friends,
But this time on earth was not all strife
We danced we sang, what a wonderful life!

To praise God above is how we spent our time
He calls us near, he says "You're mine,"
As our holy father surrounds us with love
We fear not when we rise above,

Ant there awaits a kingdom of peace and praise
We're free of guilt and shame, drama and craze,

These things I hold in my heart to be true
Our father above loves me and you,
And even if you believe in a different way
Little difference is made at the end of the day,

I want to live my life to the fullest with this comfort in mind
And I believe that in this life there is no greater gift than time,
So, take the time to say to others this
I love you and when you go you will be missed.

Written by Gloria
In Memory of her grandmother
Stella Allen Hicks
February 25, 1942 - April 15, 2016

The Decades We Won

Moons, years, and seasons past
Have come and gone but our love's last,
It's been a time since we first met
And first kiss we'll not forget,

Within our time we've both seen wars
Politicians by the scores,
We've seen ourselves in headline news
Through the happy and the blues,

We've carried each a heart to own
We hold each other to God's throne,
We take sorrows, fears and cares
To a place above and leave them there,

We've given each joys that be
Within our lives for each to see,
Of our children, friends, and kin
We're proud of them before all men,

In these times our decades saw
We strengthened each with love and law,
We've given that there is no other
Of whom we'd choose as our lover,

We love, we laugh, we cry, we sing
We toast our glass as anthems ring,
We're blessed of God and of His Son
And praise Him for the decades we won.

Democracy's Dilemma

Our politics in USA
Are tarnished thru and thru,
One side wants to cave to all
The other side, not true,

Not true to the people
But bends to one man's will,
One that seeks to rob us
Of all that we've instilled,

Now is time to cry out
For us to e'er succeed,
We must stop this madness
Of ego and great greed,

In past our forefathers
Made a lasting will,
In our Constitution
With blood and sweat and quill,

We must be reminded
That if we are to last,
Again, become united
Or Democracy is past!

The Doctrine

It took a page of doctrine
To help me clearly see,
That doctrine would not satisfy
The hunger inside me,

The doctrine spoke of "thee's and thou's"
Of what I ought to do,
It told me to be holy
It told me to be true,

It told me of my yearnings
Of what I should e'er be,
It told me of shortcomings
It helped myself to see,

The doctrine was a roadmap
It pointed out the way,
To where my heart was leaning
And what God had to say,

It told me my desires
Weren't what need to be,
But that I should seek higher
And once I find, believe,

This doctrine was my Bible
It spoke of God so free,
It took me down to bended knee
Till I found Christ in me,

This doctrine's now my mentor
I read it every day,
To know my blessed savior
And follow in His ways,

I ask you once to read it
You'll find it is so true,
That once you know this doctrine
You'll see Christ in you.

The Dreaming Hope

In hopes and dreams I see myself
In my future years,
With happiness and solace
Without great bitter tears,

I feel the winds, I see the sky
In natures truest form,
I trust that God will comfort me
Throughout life's bitter storms,

In this life I cherish things
Of present and of past,
I honor all relations true
Of things that always last,

Today I find a thing to say
Tomorrow it is true,
As dawn breaks for everyone
For me, and so for you,

Let God have the glory
For all we have to see,
And let our lives true story
Is that, in Him, we be.

Eden

The wedding day has finally come
The man I love is near,
With great respect we tie this bond
We only have one fear,

We fear our love is strongly bond
That we, each other know,
And love the same that ties us so
With it - - with each we grow,

Faithful till the end of days
We seek to be together,
To love, respect, and faithful bond
And seek to part not ever,

Within the eyes of God, we wed
He sees us in His heart,
We pray the blessings of His love
And from it not to part.

Embrace

Yesterday you were with us
We hugged you and you cared,
Today we see you laying there
And think of love you shared,

The hugs and tender kisses
The voice of sweet caress,
The times that you were with us
The things that you addressed,

The thoughts of you will never
Leave our hearts, our minds,
The times that you were near us
Left nothing else to find,

As we all still linger
In this mortal life,
We know you're with the master
Where there is no strife,

So, pray if you will for us
Our way to be quite clear,
That when we see each other
We'll hold each other dear.

In Memory of
Linda L. Kelley
1943 - 2017

Essence of a Day

I woke his morning, rushed to work
In my journey I felt a perk,
Time to wake up, time to rise
Time to see this world with eyes,

In each day in which I live
Some will take and others give,
It's not my task to ere ask why
This cycle turns with each new sky,

I give my all I give my best
From time I wake till time I rest,
In each task I find to do
I'll take the lead and see it through,

My lifestyle is my persons' best
If I'm sincere or if I jest,
With pride of life, I do all tasks
And answer all the questions asked,

In the essence of each day
The day repeats in its own way,
Though faces change and names be new
The toils of day are varied few,

My time away is time to rest
To build within to be my best,
To enjoy life as life is lived
Refresh myself with what life gives,

As all days come and all days go
This cycle turns and carries so,
Yet in all this one thing I say
It's good to have both work and play.

Eternal

Every moment passing
Within eternity,
Is memories a flashing
Of what life used to be,

My brothers and my sisters
My family and friends,
The places I would see
The times that I would spend,

Yet all that is behind me
I have no time to waste,
Nor should I e'er hurry
I never need to haste,

Eternal is eternal
No time or seconds pass,
I need not keep a journal
For here there is no past,

Within a life of sorrows
I knew suffering and of pain,
Here where there's no tomorrow
I'll not know pain again,

If you get this message
Then you will plainly see,
That sufferings are no longer
Here in eternity.

In Memory of
William O. Newman
October 19, 1937 - February 5, 2017

Every

In every moment lived
I seek to pray and give,
To give in prayer and fasting
To give to everlasting,

Every thought I think
And every time I blink,
I think to be some hero
And not to be a zero,

Every breath I breathe
I ask of God to please,
I ask to be more like Him
I'm nothing if without Him,

Every day that pass
I wonder if I'll last,
I pray to just get through it
As God will guide me to it,

Every mile I walk
I seek of God to talk,
I pray that He will be there
I ask He lead with His care,

Every line I write
I see it with my sight,
I pray that I can hear it
As God's spirit speaks it,

Every soul I meet
I ask to humbly greet,
And let them know God loves them
And rules not far above them,

Every question asked
Begs a brand-new task,
The answers are quite often
So sublime and soften,

Every prayer I pray
I guard the words I say,
I seek not to offend Him
As all resides with Him,

In this life I live
Each moment takes and gives,
Yet all is in God's Spirit
I ask - - to just be near it.

Faithful

This morn I knelt and had to pray
For God to lead and guide my way,
I read His word and took to heart
Yes, indeed this was day's start,

With opened eyes and hearing ears
I've served Him such throughout my years,
The faith in Him brings light to me
So, with His spirit I may see,

My desire's His will for me
As I would be as He'd have me be,
To give my all on all occasions
To stand for God in situations,

If I may win one thing in life
And put away the fleshly strife,
May it be He recognize
Then be a prize in my God's eyes.

Faith's Challenge

In a moment of darkness
A challenge to faith,
A sickness to healing
Of full health to wait,

A challenge in silence
A cry loud and clear,
For something to hear us
And keep us from fear,

A sickness to all
And savior to none,
We see life's ambition
What's lost and what's won,

Our spirit cries out
To shake sickness coil,
Our body refuses
To let it e'er toil,

In faith we deny
Where sickness would send,
In spirits so spry
We seek then to mend,

The life of the sickness
Diminishes fast,
We hold to the future
And all that will last,

With faith in our prayers
And prayers of the saints,
The sickness denied
It no longer taints,

Our body seeks healing
And healing takes place,
Our spirit is willing
Gives sickness no space,

The love of all life
We understand then,
Is within our kinship
Our family, our friends.

The Fall, The Rise!

In all our aspirations
In all devoted ties,
There is one meditation
In which all hope lies,

The Jesus Christ the savior
Who bled and died for men,
It's he upon who we call on
When we're distraught within,

About this blessed savior
Whose nails upon a tree,
Held him one day captive
So, he could set us free,

Free from condemnation
Free from selfish pride,
Free to daily worship
Christ at God's side,

If only we would realize
The meaning of the cross,
Was more than buying freedom
Redeeming what was lost,

The loss was in the garden
When God created man,
And set him as a master
O'er all on earth he planned,

The loss was of the spirit
When Adam led by Eve,
Ate of the tree of knowledge
And eyes began to see,

They saw the things of passion
And learned then how to lie,
And quick to accusation
Than worship God in high,

The loss was of the kinship
That God gave unto man,
To be his sons and daughters
Unto the great "I Am,"

Their loss was firmly woven
In fabric of the time,
Till Jesus Christ the savior
Would seek the lost to find,

The beauty of the savior
At Golgotha's cross,
Is that he came to save us
By dying for the lost,

Then he rose on third day
And took away the keys,
So, death it had no victory
And grave it had no sting,

Now unto this Jesus
We kneel to him and pray,
We praise him in our hearts and soul
In our remaining days,

If not for our Lord Jesus
We wouldn't understand,
That all of earth's creation
Was simply made for man,

The fall way back in Eden
Was in God's plan divine,
To raise to God a family
Of which he can call "Mine."

Family of Fortune

My family is my fortune
They are my pride, my joy,
I'm always in heart with them
It's where my soul employs,

My love for life and freedoms
Keep me thinking health,
To know of my surroundings
And what of life is dealt,

I look into tomorrow
Of what I've made today,
Surely, it's a path that
I can make a way,

All of my surroundings
My family, health, and friends,
Keep me concentrated
On where my future lends,

I accept all freedoms
They are mine to keep,
I think of them quite often
If I wake or sleep,

My family is my fortune
My health is my resolve,
My future is of certain
If I keep my God involved.

The Family of God

I have a wife and children
Of family they are mine,
I would spend more time with them
But cannot find the time,

My duties and my mission
Keeps my time at bay,
It often does elude me
Not much more I can say,

Yet there is more to family
Than just the one I have,
A family's all around me
For what God gave I have,

My brothers and my sisters
I see them every day,
I teach them every Sunday
They hear the words I say,

They see me when I'm preaching
They see me when I pray,
They see me speaking of God
And of His holy way,

This family that I speak of
Are of God's word divine,
I thank God for my family
For it is truly mine.

Family, Life, Love

In the morning when I gather
All my thoughts of family, friends,
I know not of tomorrow
Or of the day it sends,

But life is all around me
And love is in my heart,
My face is toward the heaven
And from it not to part,

This life I live is freedom
With family, friends, and love,
With every moment precious
As given from above,

To God I give the glory
For all He gives to me,
My love, my life, my family
These things to always be,

If all I have is freedom
And love within my heart,
Then life is truly precious
With family not to part,

In every moment living
To God I give my all,
For life, love, and family
He's given at his call.

The Father's Faith

We often think that faith of God
Is what just lies within,
It keeps hoping for the higher
And makes us stray from sin,

Now faith is of things hoped for
The evidence not seen,
We know the prayer is answered
Before our lips, it's weaned,

Faith in God the father
Is through his first-born son,
Faith in what we're asking
Is how the answer's won,

Faith is everlasting
It's from our heart's desire,
It brings us to God's kingdom
And raises all souls higher,

There is yet one faith higher
In all the faith we see,
That is of God the father
Who made both you and me,

He cannot tilt nor falter
He cannot once to doubt,
His spirit's everlasting
He's what all faith's about,

When we pray His favor
For miracles to be,
Far from us to doubt Him
In simpleness – believe,

Because He made creation
Of all the life we know,
Because He spans all time known
Yet sits on His throne,

Because He made life's journey
A testament of faith,
Why would we ever doubt Him?
And never seek His face?

The faith of God the father
Is always absolute,
That what He says, will happen
He is the only truth,

If we pray believing
Knowing it's His will,
We will be receiving
Our answers all fulfilled.

The Final Moments

The end of days is coming
When God will sit and judge,
All our moves and moments
The victories we've won,

He'll judge the righteous judgement
With his book of life,
Did we live in spirit?
Did we live in strife?

In our expectation
Of what is to be,
If we will just hear it
Our soul will be set free,

In the final moments
Of souls that leave this earth,
All will seek to listen
Of God, to be new birthed,

Now within this lifetime
God calls to all within,
To come into his freedoms
Escaping worldly sin,

If you get this message
Please run unto him fast,
For we are on a countdown
This world is not to last,

God is ever calling
For you to hear his name,
Give your life to Jesus
Be blessed – and born again!

The Finer Things

For every moment of living
We live for finer things,
Sometimes subdued in nature
Sometimes in what life brings,

In all our nature's seeking
Or in all of our mind's eye,
We seek to keep on living
And never seek to die,

All our work and pleasure
Brings us to a goal,
In which we have all lived for
That gives unto our soul,

All that God has given
Will take us to the goals,
Of which we keep in mind's eye
And then will make us whole.

Firm Foundation

Open hearts and open minds
I find both few and far,
Love of life and happy times
We'll find if we look far,

In times of stress and woeful days
I find that I must pray,
To God above who hears the prayer
With Him my soul must stay,

When e'er that I can find the time
To sit and still my soul,
I find that God is sitting there
To heal and make me whole,

When e'er I think amazing grace
And of His love so pure,
It raptures all my living soul
That I shall so endure,

No matter passing of the time
No matter come what may,
To my God I give my all
To end of all my days.

For My Little Friend

A little friend called Baxter
I cherished and I loved,
When he was so little
I carried him and hugged,

His hair was softly flowing
Often to the floor,
As he walked across it
Seemed to be a chore,

Always bright and playful
He'd follow and he's stay,
To see where I was going
To see if he could play,

He was my little friend, you see
Of one in which I loved,
I hope one day to see him
If God, takes him above,

He was my little Baxter
My friend, my confidant,
He was my friend thru thick and thin
I will miss him - - a lot.

*This was written for a work colleague
whose dog died.*

Ford Galaxy

Fast and sleek was thought of day
This car rolled out of Ford,
The Galaxy, they proudly say
Take us at our word,

Mine of course was second hand
And yet a few hands more,
The safety features did not stand
I knew that for sure,

One night at a traffic light
There sat a city cop,
I rolled straight thru to my fright
My brakes had failed the stop,

The cop had lights of red and blue
They flashed me from the rear,
"I hit the brakes," I told him true
He eased me of my fear,

"Go park this car, get it fixed
Don't have it on the road,
With these brakes this car's unfit"
I did as I was told.

Forever in a Dream

When my eyes behold the beauty
Of a blissful restful dream,
My soul becomes more tranquil
And my life much more serene,

Then I find the answers
To some questions never asked,
And I find myself believing
Past ideas I once had cast,

Then life becomes the living
In the things I never knew,
And I find myself forgiving
All the past I have been thru,

And the more I find the answers
To all puzzles that are cast,
Then I keep on dreaming
In a dream that ever lasts,

Then my soul's enriching
In what becomes my theme,
That life has found fulfilment
Forever in a dream.

Free Spirit

Free and clear my spirit is
With every breath I breathe,
My soul soars high unto my Lord
As in Him I believe,

My heart cries out true and strong
In what I know is true,
This savior grand died for me
He also died for you,

He did not stop at death and grave
The stone was rolled away,
He rose and lives unto this day
My soul is his to stay,

In my mind and in my heart
He lives there day by day,
I choose my words to please Him so
He will not go away,

In this life of which God gave
I trust in Him complete,
And till the end of earthly days
When He takes me to keep.

Freedom

Freedom, Freedom, Freedom
We cry it in our streets,
Freedom, Freedom, Freedom
Liberty is ours to keep,

We hear it from the places high
It's in the laws we give,
We read it in our schoolbooks now
We're taught, it we should live,

Treat all men now equally
Since created we the same,
For God has made us one and all
From Him we all had came,

But are we free from bigotry
From thoughts of "I'm the best?"
From thinking "Only I know how"
Not caring of the rest?

Truly all are special
And each has his own gift,
What to the world then could we cry
For bigotry to lift?

How long will false ego trips
Scar our nation's soil?
How will we meet this summer crop?
And how long must we toil?

The Fresh of Spirit

Upon a bended knee of prayer
I found God's spirit true,
As I prayed, it freshed my soul
It made my spirit new,

I felt him as the day wore on
His spirit guided way,
I felt His presence sure and strong
I felt it through the day,

His loving spirit kept me strong
With every breath I breathed,
I felt his closeness all day long
My inner self relieved,

When e'er I start a day with prayer
It keeps my heart attuned,
To know my God, His word so true
That He'll be coming soon,

To end my day, I knelt, I prayed
To ask Him for His grace,
For what I'd done outside His will
For sin, in Him's no place,

I prayed at night, He keep my soul
That He would undertake,
And that I find Him fresh and new
In morning when I wake,

To know of God is to know life
And of His love be in it,
A prayer to Him at start of day
Will call His fresh of spirit.

The Fresh Start

A very new beginning
A change within life's path,
A different way of living
With different living tasks,

One in which tomorrow
Is a brand-new day,
And all of my work sorrows
Will shortly go away,

Though I'll miss folks greatly
With whom I've shared my life,
There is a new tomorrow
In which, is no work strife,

One in which my living
Is simply day to day,
And I'll reap all life's giving
As I live, and pray,

In this new beginning
I hold so dear in heart,
It's more than just my living
To me, it's the fresh start.

The Friend

With every situation
Within this life I live,
We'll find that on occasion
Of things that we can give,

We can give of money
We can give of mirth,
We can give of substance
Of what comes from earth,

We can give tomorrow
Of what we have today,
We can give in sorrow
We can give in play,

In all this life of giving
One thing that will hold true,
If we give our friendship
We'll give our whole life through.

The Fun of Life

All the things I think and say
From sun to shining sun,
Are things that can be dear to me
Or things which bring me fun,

Though not always is this so
For sometimes things aren't clear,
Like deeper meanings in this life
And things that people fear,

In my life I give my all
In everything I do,
I've done so from my youth to now
And will till my life's through,

To make it simple I must say
To live your life with fun,
Enjoy the moments of each day
And then know, you have won.

From One Gone On

Looking back upon you
A word that I must say,
My life I lived was loving
As you did guide the way,

Although all days weren't pleasant
And sometimes days had rain,
I felt the love of mother
Through all the days of pain,

With the life you live now
Understand I see,
That you were always with me
Wherever I would be,

Keep this understanding
And know I am with love,
There within God's bosom
With Him up above.

In memory of:
Jimmy Doyle Hightower
August 18, 1962 – 2003

From Whence It Calls

I feel the texts are calling
To live upon a page,
I feel God's spirit drawing
Close to me to aid,

As words do hit the paper
They jingle life and rhyme,
They often tell a story
That truly isn't mine,

God knows all hearts and minds
The reader and the writer,
To give the text that stands all time
There is no calling higher,

To each that scripts the pen to page
One thing all holds true,
The words you script and rhymes you lay
Hold life in all time through,

So, know your heart and spirit true
And all that life enthralls,
Then take ye pen to page
And write from whence it calls.

Generation of Truth

As small eyes opened and first saw light
I looked in awe at the sight,
A little face with little hands
Had such a need and such demands,

As the child did rear and grow
I would impart to them to know,
Of what the world to them would be
And through their eyes, same world I'd see,

The questions asked from day to day
The times we had to laugh and play,
The lessons learned from birth to youth
The passing of the child's first tooth,

The memories made would take my mind
To yet a more early time,
What I saw within each child
So precious and so tender mild,

Is reminiscent of my own youth
As raised by one of greater truth,
She must have seen me, as I see
Of what I was and what I'd be,

Now that I am raising youths
It's mine to see them to their truths.

The Garden

In the gardens, in the valley
In the morning air,
Some are singing, some are dancing
Some have just got there,

All are hopeful, all are smiling
All are full of cheer,
All are listening to the nature
Of life and all it bears,

None the wrestles, none the weary
None the ill nor lame,
All are blissful of the season
All are glad they came,

If you wonder of the garden
Of which these pros speak of,
It's the nature of the garden
Of which has bloomed with love.

The Gift Eternal

With every Christmas present
Underneath the tree,
There is a simple present
That's shared by you and me,

A present filled with laughter
A present filled with glee,
A present for hereafter
That lasts eternity,

A present for a keepsake
A present for a friend,
A present for the future
That lasts till all life ends,

A present worth the sharing
With all family and all friends,
A present of true mending
Of all that hurts within,

This present that I speak of
Is pure and simple love,
The spirit of the season
Which holds the meaning of,

This present of all presents
Wasn't made by man,
But came from God the master
A present in his plan,

It's not of kingly riches
Nor paupers poorest robe,
It's not of hopes and wishes
But known around the globe,

It's of our hearts desire
This present to our soul,
For it will raise us higher
To know the master's goal,

It's from God's tender mercy
Given to all men,
To know God's truest nature
And of him be called - - friend.

The Glory

Every moment has its glory
Every glory has its path,
Every soul has its master
To that end the die is cast,

In the symbol of this meaning
Is a truth of all truths known,
A truth that starts "In the beginning..."
And points all towards God's holy throne,

Once a word is lightly spoken
It takes a meaning and life of own,
Whether true or lies demeaning
The word will live – its seed is sown,

With every person we encounter
We're a witness to a word,
They will know what lies within us
By the truths or lies we've heard,

If we witness for the glory
From the truths that we have known,
Then we're working for the master
Of all life, that's ever sown,

If our witness be lies many
Then the darkness we do bear,
In deceit, we lose all wisdom
And from God our souls will tear,

If I seek the moment's glory
Then I grasp the truth it sends,
If I make that my life's story
Then my time will never end,

In this life if we aspire
To know the truth of all truths told,
It will lead us to God's bosom
There to walk the streets of gold.

God is in Control

I woke to hear the thunder
The wind through bending trees,
I thought on heaven's chorus
Then I knelt upon my knees,

I heard the lightning's crackle
The rushing mighty wind,
And yet I felt a solace
An inner peace within,

In all of nature's chorus
In all the storms and woes,
My God is at the center
All outcomes, my God knows,

My solace is His spirit
My refuge is His name,
My life is His forever
My spirit He has claimed,

My God, He owns all thunder
My God, He owns all lands,
My God, He owns all nations
My God is in command,

In all my days of living
In all my inner dreams,
My God is in the center
He has woven all the seams,

So, when you hear the lightning
And when you go through storms,
Know God is at the center
From Him all life has formed,

Understand the wisdom
That God is in control,
Regardless of the lightning
And how loud the thunder rolls.

God Is...

The God of our father
The God of all time,
The God of creation
The God of all minds,

God the creator
God of love,
God of mercy
God is above,

God is within
God is below,
God is yet near
And in universe throws,

God is e'er lasting
God's always been,
God's in our fasting's
Yet never in sin,

God the redeemer
Of what was once lost,
Gives to us mercy
With his son on the cross,

God is here with us
As we seek to pray,
God's in our future
He's in everyday,

God is almighty
God is all truth,
God is a spirit
God is yet youth,

God's always caring
That we may live,
Within his statutes
And to him - - us give,

God is eternal
With no ending days,
God's our creator
With marvelous ways,

God is our father
God is our guide,
With him we're saved
If in him, we hide.

God to Guide

Once, twice, third time true
I prayed a prayer from youth,
I prayed to know the God of all
I prayed to know his truth,

I asked for God to guide me
And lead me on my way,
I asked my God to hide me
In his word to stay,

I asked him for his spirit
That I may know it new,
I asked to never fear it
I asked he hold this true,

I look unto the savior
I look unto the cross,
I look unto Lord Jesus
And ask I not be lost,

In his spirit's wisdom
He's given unto man,
The simplest directions
To one day with him stand,

To stand among the angels
As he says "Well Done,
You've took my words to spirit
Eternity you've won."

God, Family, Friends

When I see my family, friends
I know just who they are,
I love them and I know them
From me, they're never far,

I love them and adore them
I keep them in my heart,
I pray that God will keep them
That's where they all did start,

From God's Holy Spirit
Is where we all derived,
And with his spirit's guidance
To Him, we will arrive.

God's Calling

In prayerful meditation
Sitting on a pew,
I speak unto my savior
About a chosen few,

I pray for all its members
To take a willing stand,
To stand up for the upright
To help to heal this land,

As I pray, I wonder
Who will hear this call?
To pray that God will bless us
Considering how much we fall,

I've come to a conclusion
Just each time I pray,
We pray to God's own calling
And let Him lead the way.

God's Desire

Here upon my heart of prayer
I met the Lord therein,
I prayed of how we're distant
I prayed He take my sin,

I could not imagine
What kept me from His heart,
I did not see the problem
Nor where I should start,

From me it was hidden
As if I could not see,
What kept me from His presence
Was deep inside of me,

Then it came a sudden
Of all my soul's despair,
I held one thought more higher
Than God, within my prayer,

I sought that of perdition
And not God's spirit's goal,
And held the thought more higher
Of which had vexed my soul,

God's spirit over-ruling
Showed this thought to me,
I asked of God to cleanse it
That in Him I'd be free,

I sought His heart's desire
To know his inner soul,
To know my God of wisdom
His will to be my goal,

I felt His heart's desire
I held it e'er so close,
To set my heart on fire
And desire Him the most,

I then saw my weakness
Of where I had gone wrong,
I held a thought between us
Of what did not belong,

I felt His tender spirit
As He led me higher,
To know God's inner spirit
Delight in God's desire.

God's Feast

Glory in the highest
The greatest of all kings,
That would be Lord Jesus Christ
And that to us he brings,

A recipe for life he has
The base of which is love,
This course continues as
We worship him above,

With great care has he provided
This feast his spirit shares,
To all his family members
Of whom he greatly cares,

The feast is set within our hearts
The items are his gifts,
With each taste that we indulge
Our spirit soars and lifts,

A cup of love, two cups of joy
A dash of patience too,
All sprinkled with humility
And a pinch of humbleness or two,

God's feast is always with us
His ever-caring hands,
Have made the meal to all it yields
Through time and in all lands.

God's Mind

Every day we look and see
The skies above so heavenly,
We hear the birds, we see the trees
We see all nature, we believe,

In our heart's we say a prayer
A prayer to God "God are you there?"
We ask He show His love so bold
We read His book, the stories told,

We ask He lead us day to day
We look, we ask, and then we pray,
We open selves to questions asked
We give to selves our daily tasks,

We hear God's voice within our heart
We ask Him that to never part,
We know He's there, has always been
We ask He keep us from daily sin,

The point of all that's said and done
Of God, the prophets, and of God's son,
Is that one day we'll turn and see
God has His hand on you and me,

Our questions asked of what we'd know
Were answered yet some time ago,
All we need is simply hear
The words of God without fear,

God is with us, He always was
His awesomeness is what He does,
To us He gives a clarity
That life itself is where He'll be.

God's Plan

The love of God is eternal
It pulls and tugs the heart,
His spirit always pure
We never wish it part,

His mercy e'er enduring
To thousands of His own,
His kingdom o'er all ruling
From heaven and His throne,

His patience ever lasting
All time within His care,
His blessings ever casting
His own to glory share,

His statutes draw us nearer
To whom He'd have us be,
As in our hearts we hide them
For they will make us free,

The truth of our beginnings
Is from His very heart,
So that our soul's winnings
Is that which God did start.

God's Present

Long ago in a manger
A young one was born,
And though life was short
It was first Christmas morn,

There gathered angels
To view this event,
To redeem all mankind
God's son He had sent,

Now each year we do honor
With few days of our lives,
That blessed birthed morning
And His life's sacrifice,

With presents and family
We all gather around,
And give gifts of friendship
And are merry in sound,

We open our hearts to
All charities close,
We give to each other
What's desired the most,

With all celebrating
We must keep in mind,
The birth of the savior
God's present through time.

God's Respect

God respects no persons
But honors those that honor Him,
He lifts souls to His spirit
And ties them to His calm within,

God has righteous judgment
To judge according to His plan,
He is a God of mercy
He gave His Son, for every man,

God is Lord and Master
All creation by His voice,
The heavens are works of His hands
And of His spirit gave us choice,

God is all eternal
With no begin or end of days,
His kingdom fast forever stays
The wise do look to know His ways,

God is in His people
He hears their prayers and praises sung,
He cares for them from sun to sun
For them His Son on cross was hung.

God's Sigh

Throughout this life we work for
Approval without, within,
From those who have great wisdom
From those that dwell in sin,

We seek to be rewarded
For smallest of our deeds,
We seek to hear the praises
Our ego there will feed,

We have degrees and trophies
Marking our met goals,
Then others write about us
Which makes us feel quite whole,

From time of early childhood
Till we have reached old age,
We seek to hear the praises
With each life turning page,

Yet sadly sometimes missing
The greatest praise of all,
One that no one else hears
And no reporters call,

The praise of all the ages
Since the dawn of man,
A praise from the master
Of praise of every land,

A praise that has no ending
A praise that always was,
A praise with no meaning
Of what another praising does,

A praise from God the master
Who watches us from high,
A praise of love and laughter
A praise of God's approving sigh.

God's Touch

In all of our frustrations
In lifelong hopes and dreams,
In sordid situations
In sorrow's awful themes,

We find a hesitation
To openly approach,
Each change within our senses
We cautiously encroach,

Our spirit gives a warning
To look upon with care,
To look at every angle
To see if trouble's there,

Without us ever knowing
Why our spirit's so,
God has given to us
His spirit for to know,

God is ever present
In all we ever do,
His spirit will guide us
And see we make it through,

Now all this not withstanding
That we must know the Christ,
Who reaches for our spirit
He's bought us with a price,

The price for our salvation
He has paid the bill in full,
To know this blessed savior
And his spirit wonderful,

We give our hearts to Jesus
We give our souls to God,
We recognize the master
And his approving nod,

When e'er we feel this feeling
That God is very near,
We know we're with the father
And nothing is to fear,

To sum it up in essence
The feeling's in our soul,
Are feelings that the master
Has given for His goal.

God's Might, God's Glory

Stars are spinning out in space
Throughout time all will race,
To positions in God's sky
We may never know just why,

Why do lights shine above?
Why does God extend His love?
Why are we just here today?
Why don't we e'er just kneel and pray?

All that God has made and done
All His might has conquered won,
All time's essence in life's grasp
All that's known and all that lasts,

God has answered if we hear
Of His spirit so kind and dear,
If we choose to take His path
All is answered - - all will last.

God's Voice

Today I heard a calling
A voice spoke soft to me,
I knew it was from God above
Telling me, that He sees me,

I heard His voice so tender
Yet from within His word,
It summed up, within my eyes
All that I had heard,

This voice, it rang straight through me
Its essence took my soul,
It gave my heart sweet liberty
I felt that I was whole,

It sang a song in silence
Yet loud within my heart,
It took me back to memories
When my faith, first did start,

This voice I heard was loving
Pure within God's realm,
It let me see the ship I sail
That God was at the helm,

If you hear a calling
Listen very close,
Let your voice fall silent
Of God's voice - - listen most.

Going Home

I have roamed throughout life in joy and sorrow
I have toiled with my hands all the day,
I have worked and stored for a great tomorrow
I have weighed every word that I'd say,

If you're hearing this note, listen closely
For it carries a tune to the heart,
It's a note for the weak and disparaged
Keep its meaning and never let it part,

If you think upon death, life is over
Then you've missed all the clues, why we're here,
There's a God who's created all life living
We're to seek and obey with joy and fear,

Now I may not be there to remind you
To seek God in your life for your soul,
I have left and am on another journey
I am travelling to God and going home.

In Memory of
Bert Jackson
Passed on May 3, 2019

Grandpa Hicks

As there he lie in gay apparel
On we look and death we see,
But think we not of angel's herald?
For there his spirit be,

We have with us his memories
His life on earth here past,
On us he looks from Heaven's heights
He scales the heavens vast,

We look and weep while his body sleeps
King Jesus has his soul,
For in last breaths here in time
He searched out Heaven's goals,

His time on earth threescore and ten
Plus, five... a few days more,
Now in eternity we see
He stands at Heaven's door,

Sometimes we do not understand
Why death will take a toll,
But this we will now understand
It cannot claim a soul.

In Loving Memory of my Grandfather
Roscoe B. Hicks
Deceased May 20, 1983

The Grind

I wake in hours of morning
From resting sleep at night,
To meet each day's forthcoming
Which comes with morning light,

In bustling hours, I travel
To meet the deeds of day,
To do what I am trained for
To earn my living's pay,

I find my day in passing
With challenges I meet,
I conquer them with wisdom
And training that I keep,

At evening I must travel
Back to my place of rest,
To find my time of recharge
And meet the next day's test,

This cycle e'er continues
Yet all days aren't the same,
Some are filled with laughter
Some are filled with pain,

I find in moments passing
All things that come my way,
Make me that much stronger
In what I do, I say,

In wisdom there's a virtue
I see it every day,
Its merits are e'er bursting
In time that comes my way,

The essence of life's meaning
Is not just what we do,
But how that we'll approach it
In what we say, we do,

This life that we are living
Is more than daily tasks,
A chance to prove the wisdom
In all our time that lasts,

In all that I am saying
Please keep this in mind,
A life is worth the living!
It's not just daily grind.

Hallowed Ground

I knelt in prayer to pray a while
To feel God at my side,
To Him I give obedience
In Him I would abide,

I feel Him near me as I pray
As I lay down to sleep,
I ask Him to be always near
And of my soul to keep,

I feel His pleasure in my speech
When I observe His will,
My soul both worships and it fears,
I ask my will to kill,

I seek not to know my will
But rather be of God's own,
I seek to please this master grand
And praise Him on his throne,

In mortal moments as I live
I seek of His desire,
To know His spirit and His love
I pray this will transpire,

I hold dearly of His truth
His will He holds in trust,
I seek it be within my soul
To Him, to serve I must,

God is in the breath I breathe
And every living thing,
I give Him all my servitude
And with it joy I bring,

If every moment of my life
Was just to please this king,
Then joys in song would swell my heart
And to Him I would sing,

For God has granted treasure true
In what his spirit brings,
My love, my life, my soul to Him
Lord, Christ, the King of Kings.

The Handmaid's Virtue

Open to engagements
Solid in her path,
This wonder of a woman
Did things, that in life, last,

Her strength of dedication
To love, to life, to faith,
Kept her ever stronger
Till she sees heaven's gates,

Her humbleness in caring
Her love to make things right,
Her joy in helping others
Her faith to win a fight,

Her joy in hearing music
Her joy to sing a song,
Her jubilance in laughter
Will keep her memory strong,

In life she never faltered
To help one on the way,
To be a better person
This is a gift she gave,

Her mothered way of caring
For those who were in need,
The life she'd find in sharing
Her absence from all greed,

This woman that I speak of
Though born of mortal man,
Was godliness in nature
And always took a stand,

She gave in life to many
To fill the yearning need,
To all those she found captive
She helped them then she freed,

Now her visitations
Are with our God on high,
Where her needs are fulfilled by
God's approving sigh.

Happy Birthday

Happiest of birthdays
And to one that's not so old,
Please read this greeting closely
Pray you read its story told,

You are just one year older
But youth within you still,
Is constant ever growing
Reviving you at will,

This day to you is special
Holding thoughts of joy,
Delivering its message
And all that it employs,

Yesterday has passed you
Gone and far away,
Lingering no longer
Out of mind today,

Reach now for the future
It is in your grasp,
Always there before you
Doing what you'll ask,

As with every birthday
New things come with bliss,
In our eyes the presents
Enjoying birthday wish,

Lifting high our spirits,
Loving all the day,
Enraptured that the moments
Now have come our way,

Our thoughts of birthday wishes
Never seem the same,
Not that we don't ponder
Why we play this game,

Enjoying birthday passion
Is what we seek of day,
Loving birthday's season
Enjoying all the way,

Really all this note says
Lightly to the soul,
Of every birthday moment
Vivaciously to hold,

Each second of day's passing
Draws the day to end,
And all our birthday wishes
Do end and start again.

Happy Birthday!

Haylie Dawn Pruitt

How very wonderful was the day
A blue-eyed girl came my way,
Young and sweet as she could be
Love was all my eyes could see,
I love you more each passing day
Each day though you grow away,

Daddy's little girl is growing fast
And now starting school, it will be a blast,
Wondering what your life will be someday
Nana will love you all along the way,

Pretty as you can be
Raring to go, to find, to see,
Unsure to what the future holds
It's certain, life will test your goals,
To every day in which you live please do your very best
Take time for God with all you do and give to Him the rest.

.

He Lives

Thousands of our years ago
Was one - the Jesus Christ,
Of whom was born the Son of God
And Peter denied Him thrice,

He had such power to heal the sick
And of the dead, He raised,
He took transgressions from our lives
And of our souls He saved,

To a torture He was cast
To die upon a tree,
This was done to free our souls
To all that will believe,

From the death He rose again
And let apostles see,
He was Christ the Son of God
To hear, to touch, believe,

He gave such power to His kin
That they will do great deeds,
He gave the Holy Ghost within
That to the soul it feeds,

Every soul from then till now
Could witness His great power,
In claiming Him the Son of God
And being saved that hour,

In death defying moments now
Some souls will hold Him close,
Realizing that God has the power
O'er life which holds the ghost,

In every nation's prayers to God
God hears them through His Son,
O'er life, death, hell, and grave
Christ has the victory won,

To know this Christ is to know God
And all that He will give,
And knowing Christ, is knowing life
Cause in this life - - He lives!

He Reigns

In the heavens up on high
Sitting on the throne,
Watching angel spirits' fly
Claiming us His own,

Prayers to answer, hearts to mend
Holding us so dear,
Giving birth to us again
With Him we'll be quite near,

Instilling statutes in our hearts
Of what is of His essence,
Comfort guiding us, His own
As we are in His presence,

Calling us to know His will
That we won't stray nor wander,
From that perfect word of God
Nor from His kingdom yonder,

Reigning from the heaven's vast
His spirit calls our souls,
As He in us and us in Him
To make us all one whole.

The Here Beyond

The journey of this life begins
The moment we are born,
We make our family and meet friends
From both we're sometimes torn,

We grow in solid unity
We make our family proud,
We let them know they are loved
We cry this long and loud,

We'd have them all know we are here
And that they'll plainly see,
Who we are and what we've done
And know what we believe,

When time comes, a fateful day
In which we leave this life,
We hope in tears our loved one's years
Have made them safe with Christ,

To us they're gone, we cannot see
If they still remain,
We cannot see their spirit near
Nor feel their love the same,

God will keep their souls with care
For to Him they have gone,
And yet we seldom realize that
Their spirit lingers on,

God is all around us all
From Him we cannot flee,
The spirits of our loved ones gone
Are with God eternally,

With that in mind they are still here
And yet they are beyond,
For God is just a breath away
And so, of those we're fond,

We know that all God holds is true
To those within his grace,
The spirits of our loved ones gone
Are with God in His place.

The Heart of God

We ask of God, we seek and pray
Of him, in faith we find our way,
We seek his truth through Bible page
We seek to thwart the sinful wage,

Our hearts within, know of his care
We live to give, we live to share,
We give to those whom are in need
And of the poor, we clothe, we feed,

We hear the cries of those amiss
Of those in pain, or in prison lists,
We seek to calm and not destroy
We seek God's will, of it employ,

All that's listed of what we seek
Is for the truthful and the meek,
To take God's will, and of it, own
To praise and serve him on his throne,

Of praise to God, is first serve man
Of every need in every land,
To praise the God of all creation
We must fill needs of every nation,

Praise cannot be just from our lips
But of our deeds as we equip,
To meet the needs of fellow man
In every nation, in every land,

To love our neighbor as ourselves
To give in love, and not what sells,
To love our God, we must give space
Away from selves - - to human race,

If our hearts be unto God
And of our feet, be spirit shod,
Then we must know that in God's heart
We all are there - - and were from start!

✦

The Heart of Right

Holding to the rule
Making right of right,
Using every tool
Keeping things in sight,

Caring for the one
That has no one to care,
Sharing what is won
To those with none to share,

Keeping constantly
The moments and the time,
Perfecting in the sun
The prose, the words, the rhyme,

Holding on so dear
The thought of helping man,
Staying of good cheer
To be the one "am,"

Keeping all the thoughts
On moving straight ahead,
To see what time has bought
And put the past to bed.

His Guiding Hands

A heavy breath, a beating heart
I feel the words of sky,
The atmosphere both thick and clear
I know not the reason why,

A moment in my dark despair
I feel the twisted pain,
I reach to God and pray to Him
To not know this again,

The moments of my darkest hour
Brought me into light,
To know that God is ever near
And now I know His might,

He reaches out through my despair
To hold me in His hand,
He makes the storm to cease and pass
By words of His command,

I feel anew with my Lord
He brings my soul to rest,
He gives me hope, He gives me joy
Through this living test,

I always shall bow down to Him
He sets my soul at ease,
It's He who guides and cares for me
To Him I seek to please,

When e'er I feel the sinking sands
That in this life can be,
I'll hold onto His guiding hands,
Of He who sets me free.

His Lamb

The Lord is my shepherd, I shall not want
Except to be close to His spirit:
To know His goodness and kindness in strength
To know His love and forgiveness immense,

To know of His values, His statutes, His love
To know of His angels which descend from above,
To know of His mercy, His virtue and truth
To keep in His standing as I have from my youth,

To worship and praise Him each day that I live
To simply adore Him, my heart to Him give,
To honor the father of all space and time
To know that He loves me, His mercy is mine,

To give Him my being above all I know
To be His dear daughter, as He tells me so,
The Lord is my shepherd, and I am His lamb
I give all my life to the "I am, that I am."

Note: This poem was written for a specific person, not to be named within this book, hence the words '...dear daughter...' on line 14.

His Will

Happy, happy, happy
Am I of God this day,
For He sees my spirit
His love has come my way,

I talk to Him in morning
For He is at my side,
I pray to Him in evening
That there He will abide,

I know Christ is my savior
And risen from the dead,
I know He knows my worries
And all within my head,

To Him I give praises
That stammer from my lips,
In utterance and phrases
And hands of which I lift,

It is my dedication
To give my Christ my all,
And that of in my family
To Him they all will call,

I cannot make it clearer
Of why I feel this way,
That every fiber in me
Does seek His will to stay.

The Holy Gate

In all of future's future
In all the past of lives,
There is a great hereafter
In which there is no strife,

A place where is no evil
A place where is no sin,
A place that does not have masters
A place where all are kin,

A place where there is wisdom
A place that does not die,
A place where we'll see Jesus
And never tell one lie,

A place of purest scenery
Where colors burst with bold,
A place of children's laughter
A place where are no old,

A place we'll not remember
Of all that we know now,
A place that keeps all members
We just don't know how,

A place that never worries
Of weather's weary storms,
Nor of changing seasons
One season is the norm,

A place where all that enter
Will never see ill fate,
This place to you I speak of
Is just past Heaven's gate,

A place where all is holy
From dawn to breaking day,
Where none shall ever wander
Nor wish to go away,

Where splendor is all seasons
Of which our souls will wait,
For the time that's coming
Inside the Holy Gate.

The Holy Priesthood

Every moment in my mind
I have a prayer I seek to find,
A new petition to the King
An acclamation I must sing,

I pray the people see in me Christ
I pray to God to pay the price,
That to His name I give my all
As from the time I heard the call,

My prayers in kind to that end
Will of my life for God to bend,
To bend a knee in sincere prayer
To bend my will and see him there,

Perhaps my will I need not bend
But of my flesh desires end,
And hold His spirit and His truth
Above my life, in age and youth,

To give to God all moments true
Hold nothing back of old or new,
That Christ be all my spirit needs
That to the flocks through me He'll feed,

I take this not of oath of light
But trust in God, His spirit's might,
That to his name I live, I die
And of His will to ask not why,

For of His purpose, we are to be
Of His glory we will see,
Of His family we are in
We seek His will, to abstain sin,

His merits high, His statutes tall
His holiness, His grace for all,
His love for man, His plan ahead
His mighty word to us He said,

To give to Him is not a task
But rather love, that He would ask,
To know his heart, His spirit dear
To keep it fresh, in our heart clear,

To be His own, is to be called
From this life of sin and brawl,
To know his faith unto the end
And of our God to be called "friend!"

The Home of Homes

Today I found a new place
To hang my hat and things,
A place of new surroundings
A place that tranquil brings,

A home for all the weary
Yet are no sickly here,
A place that is not dreary
A place where is no fear,

A place that all tomorrows
Are in a single day,
A place that knows no sorrow
A place that will not fade,

Today I found a new home
It seems quite right to me,
From this place I shan't roam
It's where I'll ever be,

This place is for all passing
That never more they roam,
It is in God's great casting
It is the home of homes.

Honor of the Name

I gave a hand in marriage
So many years ago,
Of course, it's to my loved one
That much I do know,

This marriage to my honor
Of one I took his name,
I made it be my own
And now we are the same,

My friend, my best, my lover
This person is to me,
And if there is another
That person I can't see,

Not for lack of interest
Not for guilt or shame,
Not for miles of distance
But honor of the name,

If my honored interests
Keep my soul from flame,
Then honor I that interest
In honor of the name,

If my soul is weary
And seeks another flame,
I must stay with the honor
The honor of the name,

Though my heart may wander
My thoughts be far away,
Though my soul be restless
I'll honor in the name,

This I say in wisdom
When e'er you take a name,
Be sure it fills your wishes
And honor in the name.

The Hope of Dreams

If I were to dream of hopes
Hopes would fill my night of rest,
Are restless dreams e'er full of hope?
Dreams may take this to a test,

And when I lay in restful dream
Dreams will make my hopes so real,
Are there any dreams of hope?
Hope can cause my soul to feel,

Then I wake from restful dream
Dreaming of my inner hope,
Is it not a thing to do?
Hoping that my dreams evoke,

For every dream there is a hope
Things we wish to do,
Of the dreaming hope we wish
Tomorrow will be true,

When e'er I dream in colors grand
Tomorrow becomes brighter,
Begins with rest, and hope assured
With joy, my heart is lighter,

Dreaming makes our spirit true
New hope can make it grand,
Hope is what we always do
We hope to understand,

Start your day with fresh new hope
The day will then be clear,
New hope and dreams will come your way
Day that you won't fear,

Without the hope in restful dreams
Issues become more dire,
Of what I hope and what I dream
Sorrow becomes a liar,

So, when you lay your head to sleep
Keep hope in your vision,
Dreaming dreams of restful hope
Hope becomes life's mission.

Hope of Hopes

I had a hope, a dream be true
Of this life I live,
To love, to live, to e'er be true
And to my spouse to give,

In all I gave of yesterday
Of things I did not make,
I gave happy, I gave sad
There was no give and take,

Of things I thought I knew, I knew
They did not come to pass,
As hope ran out, the marriage too
It wasn't meant to last,

But hope in vain is not as is
Full life yet still remains,
Each day I see a newer hope
And all its hopeful gains,

If life is learned upon our birth
Then no mistakes we make,
But life is learned as we live
And learn from each mistake,

To that I've learned to love all life
And give each hope a chance,
To that end I'll live my days
And let life e'er romance.

The Hope

Listen to the winds blow
They're singing you a song,
Look how high the clouds fly
As they loft along,

Feel the warmth of sunshine
While standing in its light,
See the twinkling stars shine
And imagine of God's might,

Throughout this life as you go
You reap just what you sow,
You love your loved ones dearly
With them you would grow old,

Every moment of our lives
Leads into the next,
Every time we tell a lie
We make life such a mess,

Given that we're just human
Doesn't make it right,
To harm another soul of man
Standing in God's sight,

Every time we do a deed
It doesn't need to be,
Gainful to us every time
If were planting seeds,

Just realize how you look
In the sight of God,
See Him standing next to you
And then carry on,

When this life is over with
There we all will be,
Hoping God is merciful
To both, you and me.

Hope

When I was a child I sang
When I was a child I spoke,
When I was a child I played
When I was a child I joked,

When I grew in years I learned
When I grew in years I earned,
When I grew in years I loved
When I grew in years I hoped,

Whenever I pray I see
Whenever I pray I know,
Whenever I pray I love
Whenever I pray I sow,

Within my life's dream I love
Within my life's dream I know,
Within my life's dream is God
Within my life's dream is hope.

The House that God Built

Man will build a house
Supply the wife and kids,
With all the comforts there
And then look at what he did,

He'll furnish all the rooms
Make it oh so grand,
Sometimes overspend
Sometimes stay with plan,

He'll plant some shrubs and trees
Make the grass so green,
Make the pavement smooth
And sweep it till it gleams,

Then he'll make a plan
To insure all within,
To keep his vestment safe
Till his time will end,

God has built a house
We see it every day,
When we brush our teeth
Or when we kneel to pray,

It's with us where we go
From it, we cannot part,
This house that God has built
Resides within our heart,

It shows up when we smile
We hear it when we pray,
We know it by our faith
That God has come to stay,

His house, He purifies
He purges it from sin,
We feel this in our soul
When sin, our soul, condemns,

This house that God has built
Is always bursting new,
It's born fresh every day
As we worship on our pew,

God has built a house
It's in my heart to stay,
So, to Him I do kneel
With joy to Him I pray,

If God is in your house
Then find your spirit new,
Worship Him and pray
Give Him, all that you do.

I

I began my life as just a seed
I had no goals, no basic needs,

I grew till I was just a sprout
I planted roots, that was no doubt,

As I grew, I aged in time
My life became a nursery rhyme,

I had all I'd ever need
I needed little, yes indeed,

I now set firm within the earth
Which from generations my kind was birthed,

My purpose here is to serve man
To clean his air at God's command,

And though I sit and look so fine
Enjoying light of day,

I also enjoy peaceful sounds
Which often flow my way,

I hear it's said of old wise tales
That dogs are man's best friend,

I'll tell you true that plants will be
Man's friend until life's end.

I Love this Living

I love this life I'm living
In all the things I do,
From dawn to dusk I'm giving
In all of my life through,

If not for meditation
And serving fellow man,
I would not be myself
Nor be all that I am,

So, if you see me giving
Of what I love to do,
Just know for sure I'm living
In all I like to do.

In a Day's Work

In a day I work
I keep a pace,
I'm on my feet
From dawn till late,

I make my rounds
To all that need,
Of what I do
And who I see,

I make real sure
The work is done,
Before I rest
The day is won,

After rest
It starts again,
Another day
For it to win,

To give myself
To win the day,
Before I rest
Before I play.

I Praise God

I praise God in the morning
I praise God in the night,
I praise God in the noontime
I praise God with my might,

I praise Him with my spirit
Humbled to His will,
I praise that He is near me
My days of praise are filled,

I ask Him just to guide me
To know the more His name,
I ask He be inside me
So that I may speak His fame,

I ask my dear Lord Jesus
To stay within my heart,
I ask to never stray from
Or of His spirit part,

I praise God in the silence
I praise Him in the rain,
I can't wait till tomorrow
When I'll praise my God again.

I Promise You

Within my heart and in my head
I hold you close there to,
In the moment that we wed
We become me and you,

Now in my eyes I see you there
And feel you in my heart,
I hold you close I hold you dear
And never wish to part,

I promise you that we will be
Together throughout time,
To hold each close and hold each dear
To call each other "mine,"

I promise you that I'll be true
To hold you till life's end,
And in our journey, you will know
You're my best of friends,

I promise you our love will grow
We'll be forever true,
I promise you that we'll know
Each other thru and thru.

I Raise

Oh, dear Lord here on my knees
I raise my hands for you to please,
I kneel in prayer; I know you're there
As I raise my praise to you,

Throughout my day I've been in prayer
To know you're close, to know you're there,
I reach for you, in all you do
And I raise my praise to you,

Each night I sleep, I ask you keep
My soul at rest and thru all tests,
That I may know your spirit whole
And I raise my praise to you,

In life I seek to e'er be meek
And give you all my spirit seeks,
To praise your name, to tell its fame
And I raise my praise to you.

I Read

A line within a book
A read between a line,
A story never told
A masterpiece in time,

A novel of the soul
A text that makes me new,
A word that makes me live
A part of what I do,

I read of poet's thoughts
I read of obscure times,
I read of things life's caught
I read of nursery rhymes,

I read of journals new
I read of stories old,
I read of paupers' lives
I read of streets of gold,

With everything I do
I find the time to read,
It makes my life anew
And of my soul it feeds,

I read of what I can
And enjoy every line,
I find it is a strength
For reading builds my mind.

I See Love

I see love when ere I thinking
Of nature's truest form,
Because it's from our master
Who made all living forms,

In cloudy skies the beauty
Of nature's healing hour,
That stays the thirstful droughtness
And brings the coming shower,

The flora and the fauna
That takes each breath we breathe,
And gives to us the living
The breath of air we need,

Of all that lives and feeds of
With its sacrifice,
To keep us and sustain us
In this realm of life,

And every ocean creature
Of which we bring ashore,
They give us breaded tidings
Until we reach for more,

Of these cycles turning
I understand and see,
That they are just a message
Of what life is to be,

From Adam in the garden
Who walked in hand with God,
To Moses and commandments
Which gave the rule of rod,

Unto the revelations
Which tells us of the end,
Till in the resurrection
Christ tells us, foe or friend,

I see love in the beauty
Of all that God has made,
I see it in God's rapture
When all of this will fade,

I see love in God's kingdom
Of which, will never end,
I see love in God's family
For they are truest kin,

All and all I see love
From God, as it transpires,
I see it in his spirit
Of which there is none higher,

I see it in creation
That he has made to be,
And all I pray in seeing
Is to see it yet, in me.

If I Were Home

If I were home I'd be with friends
I'd see all family,
If I were home I'd see a field
I'd know every bush and tree,

If I were home I'd be known by name
All would see me true,
If I were home I'd be the same
As seen by even you,

I'd be no different than I am
Yet feel a bit secure,
There with family and friends
Would be a soulful cure,

But home is where I make it
And now two homes I have,
One with family, friends, and kin
The other is where I am.

I'll Love

I thought a thought
I thought it clear,
I thought to be united
With one that holds me dear,

I once was there
With love and trust,
Great compliments
And youthful lust,

We were a team
This man and I,
But time cut short
Without goodbye,

So now I seek
And yearn to live,
Of myself
My all to give,

And to receive
The like in kind,
That we will merge
In heart and mind,

I know somewhere
I'll find this man,
In all my search
I know I can,

I only ask
From God above,
This man I find
Of whom I'll love.

I'm Thankful

I looked around and took assess
Of things within my life,
Of these things I'm thankful for
My God, my truck, my wife,

My God, he gives me all I have
Of health, of wealth, of day,
He makes my life to an excess
And guides me on my way,

He lends to me great mercy
Of things both now and past,
I love to read his verses
For he will always last,

I'm thankful for my truck you see
It takes me where I need to be,
If I have a load to carry
I get there and do not tarry,

From sunup till time to sleep
I'll get there if it's high or deep,
My truck will take me where it can
I am a nature working man,

I love my wife and always have
She keeps me straight and true,
She knows my heart and knows my love
She helps me carry through,

In all the things I'm thankful for
She will top that list,
She loves the Lord and loves life true
Of me, she has the gist,

I'm thankful for my country grand
Of which I can be me,
Of God, my wife, and truck you see
I'm thankful for all three.

In Future's Fold

All my worries, my inner cares
All my sorrows, in emotion stirs,
All my yearnings, my forethought goals
All disappointments, my future holds,

Every morning, every night
Every laughter, every fight,
Every meaning, moments dull
Twilights gleaming, nights of lull,

With all sorrows, comes a care
With all laughter, love to share,
With every friendship, moments kind
With all concerns, within my mind,

We never know, what is tomorrow
When it arrives, will joy or sorrow?
All we know is what we're told
And wish the best, in future's fold.

In God's Arms

Life is such a treasure
Each day is as a gift,
Living it is pleasure
To leave it, tears a rift,

It leaves to other's sorrow
Of all that could have been,
It changes their tomorrow
Of what it held within,

It burdens hearts with heaviness
It fogs the mind with snares,
It steals away a peacefulness
And hurts the soul that cares,

But there is a different side
Of which we cannot see,
The soul that left, where it abides
Of where it now will be,

A place that holds no sorrow
Where night shall never be,
Where war and hate do not exist
A place that has no sea,

A place that holds the angels high
Where there they walk with men,
There is no sun that heats the sky
For God is there, therein,

A place that calms the burdened soul
And needs are never known,
All sickness gone and all live by
The words from God's own throne,

A place of where the angels sing
Where nothing is alarm,
And all that do dwell within
Are safely in God's arms.

In God's Eye

Did you ever touch?
Did you ever know?
The spirit of God
His love and its flow?

Did you ever see?
Did you ever feel?
The joy in your heart
And know that it's real?

In God's eye we're seen
As children of men,
He sees when we pray
He sees when we sin,

He knows our mind's eye
Our thoughts and intents,
He sees us through love
So, His son he sent,

In God's eye we're children
Not yet fully grown,
In God's eye we're learning
Of His kingdom and throne,

If we could but once
See through His eye,
We'd see everyone
To God, is His prize,

To see through God's eye
And not use our own,
Is to see everyone
And leave none alone,

It's to reach out to needs
For all of mankind,
It's to reverence the king
And see through God's mind,

In God's eye we're growing
And always will be,
But to see through His eye
Takes the faith to believe.

In Him

Every breath taken, every thought's view
All structures gone, all things anew,

All moments passing all moments within
All far away glances, all obeyance and sin,

All that is seen with naked of eye
All the stars shining in distance of sky,

All souls rehearsing the essence of life
All peaceful moments and wars full of strife,

All seasons making their way through the day
All days of breaking to night to give way,

All future and present, all present to pass
Have one connection that always will last,

Thought it be near or far-far away
All is in God - - in Him it will stay.

In Holy Valor

I thought a time to make a plea
Of thoughtful things of which I see,
To grasp, to know, to understand
Of life we live, of God and man,

I took a vow within my heart
A vow to God and not to part,
To give to God my life, my all
To listen for His spirit's call,

To teach and help my fellow man
To help him grasp and understand,
This vow, it took my inner soul
I gave to God, and came I whole,

Now I find, I look, I see
What I can do and of God please,
Not for glory, nor for gain
Not for riches, nor for fame,

Not that men should look at me
But that souls should be set free,
To please our God who holds all power
To serve Him truly, in Holy Valor.

In Memory of Vera Meiss

In all my trusted living days
I knew you as a mother,
While you were here, I was me
I looked up to no other,

You were the one that stood so still
When all around was gloom,
When folks would fear the future
For you, there was no room,

Fear was not your inner being
But love for life was cast,
Your innocence and stature tall
Will live until time lasts,

You may be gone but not to me
I never will forget,
But that these words were not relayed
Will be my sole regret,

Now that you know just how I feel
Please watch right over me,
Till in the time we meet again
With both our spirits free.

*This was written for a co-worker whose
friend/mentor passed away.*

In Their Eyes

For many years I did teach
Ones of youth, their minds to reach,
To let them see, to help them grow
The more I taught, the more they'd know,

These little ones with opened eyes
Each day would bring a new surprise,
For as they read and really learned
My respect these ones had earned,

The beauty of a learning child
Is how they view their lives so mild,
They look to us to show the way
And have more questions each new day,

In respect of how they learned
And of the knowledge they had earned,
It should be of no surprise
That we were as God in their eyes.

Isla Mujeres

In places that I wander
Along life's busy path,
My imagination ponders
A place I've spent in past,

This solitary island
In the heart of sea,
Silences my anguish
Leaving me - - to me,

Alone or with a loved one
Might you find the time,
Underneath the sunshine
Just keep this in mind,

Everything is peaceful
Resting—watching waves,
Enjoying every moment
Sure beats working days.

Jasmin

My little jewel my dearest friend
My watch mate in my life,
She kept me warm and made me smile
And kept me in her sight,

She never stood abandoned
His dearest friend to me,
And it was not at random
How our friendship came to be,

Her life was sadly shortened
But her memory never fades,
To me she was so important
I always stood amazed,

Though sadly she has parted
Yet I had richly gained,
Her time in life of friendship
The closeness that it framed,

Always I'll remember
Her antics, moves and smiles,
My dearest little Jasmin
She rests and sleeps awhile.

Note: This poem was written for a friend/coworker, at her request, concerning her pet that passed away.

Jimmy

For every sound there is a praise
For every silence a prayer,
For every speech there is a mouth
For every message a bearer,

For every time we look and see
God's grace, his love everlasting,
There is a time that our souls did seek
His face with prayer and fasting,

For every moment we live on earth
We live - we breathe - we love,
For every blessing we feel God's love
And know he watches above,

From time of birth, he leads us on
To that which brings us close,
Close to his spirit, close to his love
To what he desires most,

For every time we sing his songs
We fill our hearts with gladness,
We seek to attain abidance in
His dwelling where is no sadness,

For every day he gives to us
We place in it yet our all,
For there are days in which we can't
Of our own - heed his call,

For such times there is a need
For strength from friends and kin,
Without which we would no doubt
Lose track of where we've been,

A prayer of hope - a friendly chat
A place to spend a rest,
For every time we help another
We've passed in this life's test,

Our prayers for one that's dear to us
Agree in humble spirit,
That God sees Jimmy near to us
And of his ailment clears it.

John Ward

A friend of mine passed away
He fought for life till last of days,
His spirit challenged sickness toll
Till last of days, his spirit bold,

Notwithstanding let me say
He was the same every day,
He had a strength and hearts desire
That made one move, set things to fire,

A friend was he to many men
A worker true was he within,
To grab a task till it was done
And see it thru from sun to sun,

Indeed, a man that you could trust
His honesty, it was a must,
To tell a lie, he did not know
Integrity, kept him so,

He may be gone and, in our hearts,
A hole is there, of friendly parts,
Enriched are we to once have known
Such a man that held his own,

We hope, we pray that God will find
This friend of ours and treat him kind,
For one day we hope to see
Our friend again, in eternity.

The Labor of Love

There are lifetime moments
When all creation stills,
It's during mother's labor
Her lifetime wishes fill,

The meaning to this reason
Is of the heart's desire,
To disregard the labor
In love of something higher,

The time is near an ending
Of all the labor pain,
A time of new beginning
A season that will reign,

A time when all that matters
Is what the labor brings,
That will be loved and adored
And softly voices sing,

A time when children's contents
Are scattered ore the floor,
And parent's hearts are content
When children ask for more,

The labor of the evening
And partial of the day,
Marks that new beginning
When children come to stay,

The love of panful labor
Is seeing face of child,
Of whom the mother bonds with
So boldly yet so mild,

When she meets the labor
She then greets the child,
The rest is heaven's blessing
God's gift to tame and wild,

The meaning of this story
Is blessed by God above,
Who blesses all the living
Born of labor's love.

The Leader

I watch the channeled stations
I see the resident,
I hear his words a spewing
The tweets that he has sent,

I see he's touched on nations
And made them all our foe,
Unless he seems to prosper
His dealings take a toll,

I yearn to see a leader
That cannot tell a lie,
One who will seek after
The things we place on high,

Of whom health care will matter
Of nature he will keep,
Of retired income
He will not let it sleep,

One that chooses wisdom
In all his dealings done,
He holds his people dearest
I hope this man will run,

One who speaks with kindness
And chooses not to tweet,
Of his dearest loved ones
He chooses not to cheat,

One of whom it matters
Of words he has to say,
So, we no longer cry out
To "impeach" every day,

Of this thoughtful leader
I pray that he will be,
Here among our people
I hope soon we will see,

Perhaps within my lifetime
There will be someone,
Of which in whom I'd vote for
I pray to God he run.

The Lesson

Books I've read and books I've lost
I learned great things at higher cost,
I've learned of joy and precious things
I've learned of life and all it brings,

I've learned that learning can be fun
I've learned through learning, things are won,
No matter what I can e'er learn
Nor what that learning to me earns,

In all of life there is one lesson
To take away from all those sessions,
That best that I can ever learn
Is love of life, is born, not learned.

Let Me Be Louder

Oh Lord let me be louder
In my humble praise to you,
Let me not be a stranger
In that you'd have me do,

Let me sing from my heart
With every word anew,
Let me raise my hands in praise
And reach oh Lord to you,

Let me stand Lord in your sight
And praise with all my might,
Let me be a little louder
Oh Lord — Within your sight,

Let me kneel in humbled prayer
And know you're always there,
Let me feel your love divine
And know that I am thine,

Let me give you Lord my all
And daily to you call,
Let me be a little louder
And of myself, less prouder,

Let me stand Lord in your sight
And praise with all my might,
Let me be a little louder
Oh Lord — Within your sight.

Let me Breathe

I have one thing to ask you
Of life's necessity,
Let me stand beside you
And let me freely breathe,

Amidst the world's corruption
Among life's uncertainties,
Just let me stand beside you
And let me freely breathe,

Let me stand in my freedom
Let me breathe while freedom rings,
Let us all be seen as children
Of the God that we believe,
Let me stand up proud and mighty
Let me stand and let me breathe,
Let me breathe - - Just let me breathe

I'm not asking for a handout
I'm not asking for free fare,
I'm not asking for a dollar
Nor a cross for you to bear,

I'm not asking for a reason
Nor a thought to understand,
I'm just asking simple freedom
And beside you there to stand,

Let me stand in my freedom
Let me breathe while freedom rings,
Let us all be seen as children
Of the God that we believe,
Let me stand up proud and mighty
Let me stand and let me breathe,
Let me breathe - - Just let me breathe.

*In honor of George Floyd
Who died from police brutality on May 25, 2020.*

The Life I Love

I find my days in passing
Loving time of life,
Giving all to others
That they may have more life,

I find it therapeutic
To help folks on the way,
That thru this life of living
It helps them through the day,

Every day I wake up
I find new things to do,
To make this life of living
Good for me and you,

All anticipations
That in my life there be,
Leads me to the one thing
That I love to be,

A father to my children
A teacher to all men,
A friend to every stranger
And love this life till end.

The Life of Life

Life is simply splendid
With everything I do,
I love life in the morning
The night and afternoon,

Rainy days or sunshine
Either are so fine,
Any day I wake up
That day is surely mine,

Life is filled with colors
Spectrums from the Sun,
Life is filled with wishes
Life is filled with fun,

In life there is wisdom
Which transcends mortal man,
To be the planet's watcher
This of a divine plan,

Life is for all living
And for those soon to be,
Life is truly giving
Life gave life to me.

The Life with God

The blowing wind, the rustling leaves
The fall of life, the budding seeds,
The life that's here, the life that's gone
The living will, to those passed on,

Every moment of our life
We find a friend to care,
Of what we are and what we've done
Of our life to share,

When we pass from life to death
We can't yet understand,
Just how the passed, yet still live on
And aren't within our land,

All of nature that we see
Lives and passes on,
But souls of men are then set free
To God they all have one,

The souls don't die but live again
Within God's holy place,
In a realm we just can't see
For us, there is no space,

All of life that we know
Yet life, is more than this,
Life with God eternal lasts
The rest is hit and miss.

Life

Early in the morning,
All throughout the day,
I see things and I hear things
Of all that comes my way,

I see clouds a passing
I see the sun at rise,
I see and feel the rain and storms
I see the stars in skies,

I hear all people passing
As they go on their way,
I'll see some in hereafter
If they have found their way,

I live life every moment
As days and years pass by,
And give thanks that I live it
Without a question why,

Every moment passing
Leads into one more,
This life I live in passing
Will take me to God's shore.

Life's Tests

Having life ahead of me
Astounds me every day,
Yet a simple question is
Lurking in life's way,

Is the future my control?
Evolving with my soul?
Do I instead with times to roll?
And seek my own thought's goal?

When will all lips answers be
Nestled in my mind?
Perhaps this I shall never know
Reeling throughout time,

Understanding things, I've seen
Is paramount at best,
To know that I can understand
Teaches me life's tests.

The Light

A light amidst the ocean
It shines its beacon true,
Through mist, fog, and stormy seas
The light comes shining thru,

The peril of the rocky shores
The dangers of the depths,
This beacon leads the ships to shore
Where sailor kind are kept,

Through nights and years of shining
This beacon never fades,
But through all peril shineth
So, ships can find their ways,

As on a shining hilltop
Our Savior calls to all,
The perils of the waters
Will not make you fall,

"Just walk in faith unto me
You will not sink or drown,
I'll guide you with my spirit
Which leads to hallow ground,"

Christ Jesus is this savior
His beacon shines to all,
He'll listen and He'll hear us
If we, to Him, will call.

Little Me

If I were to be
Anyone but me,
I'd lose my concentration
I'd have no dedication,

I'd be a muse in waiting
For reality to drop,
I'd be so hesitating
Everything I'd try would flop,

If I tried to be another
To my sisters and my brothers,
They surely would not see
What could become of me,

If e'er I think to try
Of what I know is not I,
Then neve would I be
The person that is me,

So, in this life I live
And if I am to give,
I'll always seek to be
A humble little me.

The Look Ahead

In all life's natural moments
In which we live, we breathe,
We look into the future
Of what we might receive,

Will we have a family?
Will we have great friends?
Will we be together
Until life's final end?

Will we have great children?
What will be their course?
Will they be respected?
Will they be endorsed?

Will we have our freedom
Of which we all can share?
Will we all know Jesus?
Of his love and care?

Looking towards the future
Is not towards the end,
It's looking into God's love
With spirit, family and friends.

The Lord is My Shepherd

The Lord is my shepherd, I shall not want
Except to be close to His spirit,
To know His goodness and kindness in strength
To know His love and forgiveness immense,

To know of His statutes, His values, His love
To know of His angels which descend from above,
To know of His mercy, His virtue and truth
To keep in His standing as I have from my youth,

To worship and praise Him each day that I live
To simply adore Him, my heart to Him give,
To honor the father of all space and time
To know that He loves me, his mercy is mine,

To give Him my being above all I know
To be His dear daughter, as He tells me so,
The lord is my shepherd, and I am His lamb
I give all my life to the "I am, that I am."

Lord of My Soul

"As the lord liveth
So liveth my soul"

In all of God's creation
From sea to shining sea,
I know that He is with me
In all I am to be,

He teaches me of morning
He guides me through the night,
He exhorts and rebukes me
He leads from wrong to right,

I see him in my family
In many things they do,
I speak to Him in prayer room
Of choice I follow through,

I see Him in my friendships
In words we choose to say,
I hear Him in their whispers
And when I kneel to pray,

In all of His creation
I find my soul is best,
When listening to His teachings
That's where my soul finds rest.

The Lord of Souls

I've been to many churches
I've visited a few,
In my heart I am a Christian
But not just in the pew,

I know Christ is our savior
The son of mighty God,
He's also my redeemer
He dwells where angels trod,

Daily I do hear Him
He's in my heart to stay,
He knows my every worry
He hears all I have to say,

He listens when I pray now
He answers in His time,
He's given me a power
His love, to make it mine,

In this life I carry
This savior in my heart,
To know His tender spirit
And from it not to part,

If you were to be whole
Then go to Him and pray,
That to you He will listen
He will not walk away.

The Lord's Will

Many things we do in life
Defines our very soul,
They may make us empty
They may make us whole,

Self-destruction ruins our life
It kills the mortal man,
Things of grace do remove strife
These things are of God's plan,

We may find we live a life
Enjoying traits of flesh,
These things may tarry with our soul
And vex us till our death,

Of these things, we're often judged
By eyes of every man,
If it be good or it be bad
We're judged as understands,

Yet Christ did judge accordingly
Not what we did to self,
But of the deeds done on Earth
Of which, it others helped,

"Depart from me" I know you not
Was said unto the "Saved,"
Who thought that their committed faith
Would save them from the grave,

But those He chose to friend instead
Were those of whom had helped,
Of persons couldn't help themselves
And couldn't flaunt great wealth,

Christ's judgments true came with no price
Of what men thought to be,
But caring nature selfless true
Gave He eternity,

The message true in knowing God
Is not of "Thee's and Thou's,"
But of the selfless sacrifice
Of which there are no vows,

If we think that only sin
Will keep us from God's gate,
Then lost are we to know His will
We pray it not too late,

For God to judge the life of man
Is not what man has won,
But did he help the helpless man?
And of return ask none?

Do not judge a life once lived
For God is judge of all,
His judgements true and spirit rules
Is clear to one and all,

If we live a life to self
And choose to help no man,
Then judged are we of God divine
And will not to Him stand,

If we live a life for all
But still, we have a vice,
Then God will judge us for the deed
In which we asked no price,

For God is love and loves us all
Regardless of our sin,
Of which Christ paid on Calvary
To give us peace within,

And though our hearts may not know
Just when we served the Lord,
He sees our love for fellow man
And of that He rewards,

It's not our place to judge a soul
We do not know its path,
Of when it served our God on high
Nor are we priv to ask,

God's kindred be of those who served
And never sought a price,
But to them, was life's reward
And of the feeling, "nice,"

In God's kingdom there will be
Those that served His will,
Not of what we understand
But His desire filled.

In Memory of
Krystal Kay Tippett
March 28, 1984 - July 7, 2018

Loretta Nicole Fugate

Loretta, our little darling
Our heart is with you now,
Reaching to God's bosom
Embedded there somehow,

Though we dearly miss you
This we have to say,
All that we had hoped for
Never came our way,

In a fatal instant
Chaos took your life,
... to our deepest sorrow
Our baby died that night,

Loving you forever
Every heart-felt beat,
For you are in God's bosom
Under His realm to keep,

Gates of heaven opened
And there is where we'll find,
This our little darling
Eternally throughout time.

In Memory of
Loretta Nicole Fugate
April 28, 2019 - November 27, 2020

The Love of Life

Life is all among us
Living for the love,
Listening to our surroundings
Thanking God above,

Open to commitments
Giving joyous smiles,
Reaching to intentions
Going extra miles,

All our waking moments
All our dreaming bliss,
Brings life unto us
A life that we can't miss,

Once we give our hearts to
Another living soul,
Life takes on more meaning
It makes our spirit whole.

The Loved, The Missed

A brother passed away today
He will be missed, he's loved,
He fought a battle long and hard
But soon he was out gloved,

The battle took its deathly toll
It took a loving life,
One with love for all he knew
He chose to stray from strife,

With pride, my brother fought the fight
He knew he could not win,
Regardless what the outcome be
He'd fight it once again,

To life, he held a life-long love
To live, to laugh, to love,
To care for others as himself
To know of what's above,

Of life, he's on the other side
A side we cannot see,
Yet he is there, and we are here
He'll live eternally.

The Madness of Men

God created Adam, Eve
And gave to them his plan,
"Be ye fruitful...multiply"
Fill the earth with man,

"Here you have the tree of life
Eat and never die,
The tree of knowledge touch it not
Do not question why,"

Of the tree of knowledge
Both of them did eat,
That moment their lives ended
Yet time was not complete,

Noah's grace in God's eyes
Saved him from the rains,
All else living perished
Were never seen again,

Moses down in Egypt
Told Pharaoh of all truth,
But Pharaoh would not harken
He died with all his troops,

The children of one Israel
Crucified the Christ,
"Let it be on our heads
We will pay the price,"

The Nazi and the Germans
Killed millions of the Jews,
Made soaps and shades with oil and skin
And gave them history's dues,

Wars were fought for money
To gain much better lands,
To find the milk and honey
For oil in foreign sands,

Sodom of Gomorrah
Took an evil choice,
God's angels hastened on them
And then they had no voice,

In times and varied seasons
Men have taken lives,
Have killed and maimed with no respect
Had children as their wives,

In man's saddened sorrow
He turned unto great sin,
To refuse God the Father
The peace and joy within,

The choices men are making
Do not know the cross,
Nor gifts from God's own spirit
Nor reaching for the lost,

God is ever watching
The moves that man will make,
The burdens that he carries
The things that he will take,

God is always with us
But if we live in sin,
We will come to realize
The madness of all men.

The Mark of Friendship's Favor

How a man is measured
Is that among his friends,
Where does kinship favor?
Where does kinship end?

To every man there is a right
To be so true to self,
Notwithstanding his own might
To befriend someone else,

A friend is one that cares the most
Of how you view yourself,
The friend will tell you wrong or right
And if you're needing help,

A stand-up friend will know you true
And help you keep in check,
The things you do and what you say
Of days you feel a wreck,

Of all friends my life can find
I'll not find such so true,
As friends I have and friends I've known
That help me carry through.

Me

To everyday I wake
I take account of self,
I seek to be united
I seek to have good health,

My husband is my minder
He brings out all of me,
We love and we're united
To be all we can be,

My job to me is greater
Than some things in my life,
It keeps my time together
I find it little strife,

My life is filled with wishes
That most of which are true,
My love for life of wishes
Will always be so true.

The Meeting

With every day I'm living
I know that God is real,
I feel him in the morning
And when I pray and kneel,

He is ever with me
All throughout my day,
He helps me and he guides me
He makes assured my way,

I think of Christ the savior
And what he means to me,
He's given me forgiveness
And lets me e'er to be,

I love this life of living
Of where I know of God,
I know of his forgiveness
His righteous approving nod,

If you ever see me
In a moment of my prayer,
You'll know that I am with him
In prayer, I meet Him there.

The Mercy of Love

God made man to be His son
In His plan a family one,
Yet in man's day he turned from God
And God chastised with rule and rod,

It grieved God's heart that man had sinned
Made He an ark and shut man in,
All else died that disdained God
But God showed mercy with His rod,

Noah and seven then came forth
They reclaimed earth and took its course,
God placed a sign in the sky
To not destroy in days gone by,

Of God's love He so loved man
He gave His son to fill His plan,
From man's heart He could not see
All God's love and there to be,

With the Christ, the sacrifice
God made a way for eternal life,
To take man's sin and cast away
So, He judge not on judgement day.

Mercy of Stupidity

I thought I heard a rallied cry
Of something never lost,
"Unfairness" claimed deceitful cries
"Our country pays the cost,"

"Our enemies are in our house
They cannot of truth stand,
They lie, they cheat, they make things up
They're corrupt in our land!"

This cry has been four years or more
Repeating time to time,
An insult to our way of life
Deceiving hearts and minds,

In all the wisdom of our land
We've let it step aside,
To mercy of stupidity
Of which we cannot hide,

To think that we have cheated self
As a country whole,
To make believe an enemy
That steals our country's soul,

These cries we hear, have no base
No solid standing form,
But all are made of one man's mind
To tear us from all norms,

With each cry we've gotten worse
Divided we will fall,
Unless we turn our ears away
And listen to truth's call,

All our hearts and minds intent
Should be of unity,
Not thrown and thrashed in words of woe
In mercy's stupidity,

Once again, we hear a cry
To let go of this past,
To make our nation firm and strong
To be, as we were cast.

Hidden Texts

Always   pages 18 – 19:

This poem has a message starting at the top and reading the first word and adjoining comma plus the entire 2nd line in the third stanza. The message should be read as:

"Pamela,

Have a wonderful birthday season and enjoy every minute, I'm sending this message in a card, with more love than I can express in written or spoken words,

Love you always,
David"

Amina Rose Fisher   page 22.

This poem has a message using the first letter of each line and the entire line of the last stanza to read:

"Amina Rose Fisher My daughter - - I love you."

Ara Aloise Nash Friedberg   page 26.

Using the first letter of each line, this poem spells out the title:

"Ara Aloise Nash Friedberg"

Haylie Dawn Pruitt   page 150.

Using the first letter of each line spells the title:

"Haylie Dawn Pruitt"

The Hope of Dreams.   page 170.

Using the first word of each line creates a small poem:

If hopes are dreams and dreams are hope
Then dreaming is hoping for things of tomorrow,
When tomorrow begins with dreaming's new hope
We start the new days without issues of sorrow.

So, keep dreaming hope

Isla Mujeres   page 201.

Using the first letter of each line the message reads:

"I am at Isla Mujeres"

Loretta Nicole Fugate   page 228.

The first letter of each line spells the title:

"Loretta Nicole Fugate"

www.ingramcontent.com/pod-product-compliance
Lightning Source LLC
Chambersburg PA
CBHW051509120626
46551CB00012B/848